Our future is certainly uncertain, but one thing's for sure: Without young leaders we have no future. Branham has put in your hands a powerful tool with seven principles to help you coach up young leaders. *What Are You Waiting For?* is a timely coaching manual for those of us who care.

    Mark E. Moore, PhD, author of *Core 52* and Teaching Pastor at Christ's Church of the Valley.

As I read this book, I was simultaneously so inspired and yet so grieved for the many years lost to the lie that I wasn't old enough, experienced enough, fill-in-the-blank enough to be used by God. Josh has masterfully written this book in a way that will inspire, equip, and empower generations of young leaders to come. He does this through examples from his life and Scripture as well as through helpful practices for cultivating and leveraging each of the seven skills that will give our young kingdom leaders of today an edge.

    Alice Matagora, author of *How to Save the World: Disciplemaking Made Simple*

Joshua Branham may not be old, but he's got a few nuggets of wisdom blended with Scripture, experience, and a little humor for good measure that have been distilled into this book. *What Are You Waiting For?* is a book you'll actually read due to its winsome style, but more importantly, reading it will cause you to reflect more seriously on what God may be teaching you on your own journey if you have the ears to hear.

Peyton Jones, author of *Church Plantology,* Founder of NewBreed Training, and co-host of the Church Planter Podcast.

What Are You Waiting For? is a must-read for anyone who wants to break free from the "maybe when you're older" mentality and step into the leadership God has called them to today! If you're looking for inspiration and encouragement to pursue your purpose right where you are, this book is a must read. With practical wisdom and powerful stories, this book will challenge you to stop waiting for the perfect moment and start making an impact now, no matter your age or stage in life!

Hannah Gronowski Barnett, Founder & CEO of Generation Distinct, Speaker, Author

What Are You Waiting For? is a refreshing jolt of youthful possibility grounded in wisdom. This book will give young leaders both permission and direction to do the important work God created them to do.

Daniel McCoy, PhD, editorial director of Renew.org

WHAT ARE YOU WAITING FOR?

a renew.org resource

A Young Leader's Guide to Changing the World

JOSH BRANHAM

Foreword by *JAYSON FRENCH*, President of Christ in Youth

What Are You Waiting For? A Young Leader's Guide to Changing the World
Copyright © 2025 by Josh Branham

Requests for information should be sent via email to Renew. Visit Renew.org for contact information.

All Scripture quotations, unless otherwise indicated are taken from the ESV® Bible (The Holy Bible, English Standard Version®). Copyright © 2001 by Crossway, a publishing ministry of Good News Publishers. Used by permission. All rights reserved.

Scripture quotations marked NIV are from the Holy Bible, New International Version®, NIV®. Copyright © 1973, 1978, 1984, 2011 by Biblica, Inc.® Used by permission of Zondervan. All rights reserved worldwide. www.zondervan.com. The "NIV" and "New International Version" are trademarks registered in the United States Patent and Trademark Office by Biblica, Inc.®

Emphases by the author are in italics.

Any internet addresses (websites, blogs, etc.) in this book are offered as a resource. They are not intended in any way to be or imply an endorsement by Renew.org, nor does Renew.org vouch for the content of these sites and contact numbers for the life of this book.

All rights reserved. No part of this book, including icons and images, may be reproduced in any manner without prior written permission from the copyright holder, except where noted in the text and in the case of brief quotations embodied in critical articles and reviews.

ISBN 978-1-959467-42-7 (Paperback)
ISBN 978-1-959467-43-4 (ePub)

For Lily, Rosie, and Zoe.
May God give you the courage to change the world.

CONTENTS

Foreword	9
Introduction: Maybe When You're Older	13
1. Fight	27
2. Possibility	49
3. Weakness	73
4. Calling	99
5. Attention	125
6. Listening	147
7. Innovation	171
Conclusion: What Are You Waiting For?	199
Notes	209
Acknowledgements	215
About the Author	217

FOREWORD

From that MLB Prospect to NFL Draft, our culture celebrates the rookie. Our culture sees youth as the pathway for growth. And yet, broadly speaking, the Church has lagged far too long in putting the ball in the hands of young leaders. In this book, Josh sets a compelling case and a clear path for young leaders to be more than consumers; he challenges them to be contributors.

Josh addresses the quiet yet growing refrain from a young generation. They are respectfully saying to the church, "Use me or lose me." This book gives them permission to do more than attend—it gives them permission to be *activated*.

That's a lesson I've learned over 30 years of discipling teenagers—as a youth minister, as the president of Christ In Youth, and as a parent raising four teenagers. Over those decades, one thing has become abundantly clear:

WHAT ARE YOU WAITING FOR?

We've spent too long measuring the wrong things. Churches and youth ministries have treated attendance as the ultimate sign of health, but a full room of people doesn't mean we're raising disciples.

It's time to shift the metric. We must prioritize equipping and activating young leaders to live out their faith—not as passive consumers but as active contributors to God's kingdom. Josh speaks directly to young leaders, and he gives them permission to follow that call stirring in their spirit.

Josh Branham's *What Are You Waiting For?* is the handbook we've been waiting for to lead this shift. Josh doesn't just talk about young leaders; he speaks directly to them, dismantling the lie that they need to wait until they're older, more experienced, or more credentialed to make an impact. This book is a call to stop underestimating what God can do through this generation.

Josh's personal stories—of being trusted with leadership at a young age, of taking bold risks in ministry, and of failing forward—make this book a compelling read. But more than that, his insights remind us that the future of healthy leadership will come when young leaders are provided with opportunities and the resilience to take a shot. As Josh illustrates, the goal is

FOREWORD

to cultivate a culture where young people are trusted, challenged, and activated to live for Jesus.

For young leaders, this book is a great playbook for how to get started and sustain yourself as a growing leader. For church leaders, this book will inspire you to rethink discipleship in your ministry. It's not about creating more programs but about creating more opportunities for young people to lead. For parents, it's a reminder of the sacred responsibility we have to raise contributors, not just well-behaved kids. And for anyone investing in the next generation, this book is a reminder that activation is messy—but it's also where transformation happens.

I've spent decades working with young people, leading small groups of eighth-grade boys, and walking alongside thousands of teenagers through CIY. I've seen firsthand what happens when we trust young people to lead. They rise to the occasion. They change their communities. And they grow into the kind of disciples who activate others in return.

So, what are you waiting for? Let's equip this generation to lead boldly for Jesus.

—Jayson French
Parent, Discipler, and President, Christ in Youth

INTRODUCTION:
MAYBE WHEN YOU'RE OLDER

The Great Coconut Relay was a phenomenal success! Except for the one girl we rushed to the emergency room.

The relay was the last activity I planned for a junior high summer camp. The rules were simple. Teams of students would compete in a series of challenges. As soon as one student completed their task, they would run to the next station and hand off the baton (a.k.a. coconut).

Once the final teammate crossed the finish line, the game wasn't over yet. The team had to crack open a coconut somehow and eat the flesh inside. I vividly remember explaining the rules to a group of rowdy kids.

"But what if I'm allergic to coconut?" one student protested.

"I'm sure you'll be fine," I quickly responded.

WHAT ARE YOU WAITING FOR?

It didn't even cross my mind that this student was actually allergic to coconut. I thought she was raising a hypothetical concern to get out of the activity. Obviously, she wasn't required to eat the coconut to play the game, but you know how kids get caught up in the moment.

As the game unfolded, other than a mild allergic reaction, she was fine.

Why were we using coconuts in the first place?

Earlier that day, Martin (a camp director) asked if I wanted to head into town to pick up supplies for a relay race. We ended up at a bargain grocery market. When I saw a perfectly stacked pyramid of coconuts on sale, I knew it was meant to be.

After filling our baskets with the rest of the items for the relay race, we hopped in the van to head back to camp. Before we got back onto the highway, Martin pulled into Dairy Queen and told me to order whatever I wanted. I ordered a Reese's Peanut Butter Blizzard with hot fudge. Free ice cream is good for the soul.

A meaningful conversation is like lightning. You never know when it is going to strike. On the way back from Dairy Queen, I had a conversation that changed the course of my life.

"What do you want to do with your life?" Martin asked.

INTRODUCTION

"One day I would love to lead a church. For now, I plan on finishing up at college. Maybe I'll get an internship in youth ministry. Once I have enough experience there, I can start leading adults. Then once I've done that for a while, it would be awesome to plant a church. But who knows how far off that is?" My answer was very diplomatic.

I'll never forget what Martin said to me next.

"You are kidding me, right? Josh, I want you to know that you don't have to wait to do big things for God's Kingdom. In fact, I'm scheduled to preach at my church this upcoming Sunday. If you are able to stay in town after camp, I want you to preach instead."

> **YOU DON'T HAVE TO WAIT TO DO BIG THINGS.**

At the time, I was 19 years old. I had never preached a sermon. I had never even taken a public speaking class. And Martin was offering to let me preach at his church? Now *that's* trust.

To my relief, I couldn't stick around because I had another camp to be at the following week. I'm sure that sermon would have been a train wreck. In a way, that's the point. Young people need someone to trust them—even if they fail miserably.

It's hard to overstate the significance this conversation had on my life. Martin believed in me before I believed in myself. I looked at myself and saw a teenager. Martin looked at me and saw an emerging leader.

Maybe you are reading this and need someone to believe in you. You need someone to see something inside you that you're not sure is there. I hope this book can be for you what that Dairy Queen conversation was for me. Get yourself some ice cream to go with it.

"HOW OLD ARE YOU?"

As a pastor in my twenties, people asked me how old I am more times than I can count.

Sometimes the person asking followed up with a compliment about how impressed they are that I've done something beyond my years. Other times they looked at me with skepticism in their eyes as if to say, "Who put this guy in charge?" On one Christmas Eve, a lady literally said, "What are you, twelve?!"

I've often wondered how old I'll be when people stop asking. When I turn 40? When the gray hair comes in? When I am finally able to grow a beard? It might be a while.

I don't want to give off the wrong impression. I'm not personally offended that people ask my age or even that they think I'm young. But there is something troubling to me about this question. It reinforces a

INTRODUCTION

cultural narrative that says you must wait before you can do great things. I call this the "maybe when you're older" mindset.

…maybe when you finish your degree.
…maybe when you have three-to-five years' experience.
…maybe when you are older.

A trend has been developing in recent years. We live in a world where people expect less and less of young people. Teenagers enter their twenties and have trouble #adulting. People may mature in years, but it doesn't always translate to emotional or social maturity. Some psychiatrists have started using the term "Peter Pan Syndrome" to diagnose grown-ups who never really grew up.

Adolescence is getting longer. The five traditional demographic markers of adulthood (leaving home, finishing school, getting married, having a child, and becoming financially independent) are happening later than ever before. In 1960, 66 percent of American men and 77 percent of American women had completed all five of these milestones by age 30. In 2010, only 28 percent of men and 39 percent of women had done so at age 30. As Kara Powell, Jake Mulder, and Brad Griffin put it, "Fifteen is the new 25. Twenty-five is the new 15."[1] Yet I believe that young people can accomplish great things. There are natural characteristics that teenagers and twenty-somethings have that the world needs. Churches, non-profits, and businesses need leaders who can question the status quo—people too young to know better. A youthful presence can invigorate and revitalize a culture. Young leaders have strengths (at least seven; see below) that uniquely position them to change the world.

> **A YOUTHFUL PRESENCE CAN INVIGORATE AND REVITALIZE A CULTURE.**

EXTERNAL OPPOSITION

My conversation with Martin that day reminds me of the words that the apostle Paul wrote to his apprentice Timothy:

> "Don't let anyone look down on you because you are young, but set an example for the believers in speech, in conduct, in love, in faith and in purity."
> (1 Timothy 4:12, NIV)

Timothy found himself in a challenging leadership position. He was leading the church in the ancient city of Ephesus. Paul wrote Timothy to correct people

INTRODUCTION

whose lives were inconsistent with the way of Jesus. Paul also told his apprentice to implement structural leadership changes in the church. It would be one thing if Timothy had grown up in Ephesus and had a lifetime of rapport with the congregation. But Timothy wasn't from Ephesus; he was from Lystra. Not only was he an outsider, but he was young. But how young is *young*?

Sometimes when people read this passage, they think of Timothy as a teenager Paul left behind on one of his mission trips. *Home Alone* style. That's not entirely accurate. The Greek word for *young* is *neotēs*, which refers to a person of military age. In this case, *young* could be anyone aged twenty to forty. Timothy was likely in his thirties as Paul wrote these words.

The point isn't to try to figure out exactly how old Timothy was when his mentor Paul wrote him a letter. The fact is that there were people in the Ephesian church who didn't respect Timothy. They thought he was too young to lead. They were older than he, and they were convinced they knew better.

Timothy faced external opposition to his leadership. You've probably faced this as well. How can you make a difference if no one gives you a position of authority? Why speak up if no one is willing to listen to your voice? When will someone let you make a decision for once?

WHAT ARE YOU WAITING FOR?

The irony of our modern culture is that everyone wants to look young, but no one respects you if you are young.

It's frustrating to feel like God is asking you to do something big, only to be stopped short by the system, culture, or older people around you. Some young people respond by exploding into arguments with the naysayers. They think that the best way to make a path forward is to be a steamroller.

Others who are young quietly simmer in their anger. They disengage and retreat from relationships with older generations. Both of these approaches deepen generational divides and erode healthy community. The path of anger is a dead end.

Paul doesn't tell Timothy to argue or disengage. He tells him to go ahead and lead by example. Live a life that people look up to. You don't need a position, a platform, or a certain personality type in order to influence others. Often the best way to make a difference is to show people how to live through your actions.

You can build someone up with your words *today*. You don't have to wait to live a righteous life. Love your neighbor with the sacrificial love of Christ. A good leader is a person that people love to follow. If you live a life that people look up to, pretty soon people will be following you whether you asked them to or not.

INTRODUCTION

Leading by example is an often overlooked yet potent way to make a difference.

INTERNAL INSECURITY

Timothy faced another obstacle in his leadership. He was timid. We know that Timothy had a recurring stomach problem. Some speculate that this was caused by his nerves. Paul has to remind Timothy that "God gave us a spirit not of fear but of power and love and self-control" (2 Timothy 1:7). Timothy dealt with internal insecurity. Maybe he always lacked self-confidence. Or perhaps he let discouraging words of others cause him to question his calling. If you hear a lie enough times, you might begin to believe it.

The moment we declare faith in Jesus, the enemy declares war on us. Things really start to heat up when we begin to make a difference for God's Kingdom. If you're sitting on the sidelines, the devil has nothing to worry about. It's once you begin to activate your spiritual gifts that the battle begins. If the external opposition won't work against you, the enemy will try to shake your inner world.

Have you grown up around disheartening voices? Do you ever doubt that you'll do anything significant? Do you compare yourself to others and feel like you don't have any spiritual gifts? Is your personality quiet and unassuming? How secure is your identity?

It's essential that your identity is securely rooted in who you are in Christ, not in what you do for him. As a Christian, you are adopted in the family of God. You are forgiven and redeemed. You are saved by grace through faith. You are invited into the Kingdom. You have been given every spiritual blessing in the heavenly realms. All of this is true because of the gospel, before you even had a chance to say, "Thank You!"

Once we know who we are in Christ, we are ready to go into battle. I love how Paul tells us to put on the helmet of salvation. We must always keep the truth of the gospel present in our minds. It's the new reality that we live and breathe every day.

Everyone has days where they doubt they are called to do anything significant for God. I've had plenty of my own (especially when writing this book). Just know that if God called you to it, he'll see you through it.

IF GOD CALLED YOU TO IT, HE'LL SEE YOU THROUGH IT.

Paul believed in Timothy even when Timothy didn't believe in himself. We all need a Paul in our lives.

INTRODUCTION

USE IT OR LOSE IT

Have you ever started a fire with a match? It's important to delicately manage the amount of oxygen you give the small flame. Blow too hard and you'll put it out like a birthday candle. Don't give the flame any oxygen, and it'll flicker and fade. Fail enough times and you're out of matches.

Paul told Timothy to "fan into flame the gift of God" (2 Timothy 1:6). The years of your youth are a gift. On the one hand, you don't want to burn out by attempting to do too much too soon for God. At the same time, if you never exercise your faith, the fire will die out on its own. Lean in and blow lightly on the flickering flame of whatever gifts, passions, and opportunities God gives you. Give it enough time and enough fuel, and you will see a wildfire of impact for God's Kingdom. I recognize that it doesn't always feel easy to be a young person. I remember trying to get my first job in high school. I must have handed in a dozen applications for everywhere from Subway to Walmart. I didn't get a single call back. It can be hard to catch a break. You'll encounter plenty of external opposition or internal insecurities.

WHAT ARE YOU WAITING FOR?

At the same time, there are things about you when you are young that give you a youthful edge. This book will fan into flame seven skills that you can start practicing today. Some of these skills you might already possess as natural strengths. We'll talk about how even your weaknesses can be leveraged for God's purposes.

Here's the deal with these seven characteristics—they are "use it or lose it." If you don't use them when you're young, you will naturally unlearn them as you get older. It's just the way it works. The season you are in is only an advantage if you make the most of it. The ticking clock adds to the gravity of the situation. Hone these skills and you'll take them with you into the rest of your life.

Your youthful edge is like a muscle. If you train these seven skills, they will become strengths. If you do nothing, you will atrophy. It's scary to put yourself out there and try to change the world. You won't know what you're doing all the time, and you most certainly will fail from time to time. The goal isn't to be perfect. It's to muster up the courage to start trying things imperfectly. The key is to start small.

Word order matters in English. For instance, there is a world of difference between "one day" and "day one." Some people live their whole life saying, "One day…."

"One day I'll start exercising."

"One day I'll read that book."

INTRODUCTION

"One day I'll clean the garage."

If you live by the motto, "One day," it's likely you'll never get around to doing important things. The good works that God calls you to each day are much more important than having a clean garage.

Even if you do eventually get around to following Jesus with everything, think of all the years of impact you will have wasted. Imagine you wait ten years to start making a difference for God. Ten years from now, you'll largely be starting from ground zero.

We need to switch the word order to "day one."

Make today your "day one." Your impact may start small, but with God's blessing, it won't stay small. After all, the kingdom of heaven is like a mustard seed (Matthew 13:31). If you start today, imagine what God could do in a decade. Plant enough seeds and eventually you'll have a forest. The best part is that consistently following Jesus each day, starting today, enables you to see amazing fruit one day. It could happen like this:

Talk to your friends about Jesus today. One day, they come to Christ.

Pray for the lost today. One day, see revival.

Donate toward missions today. One day, become a global missionary.

Serve in church today. One day, plant a church.

WHAT ARE YOU WAITING FOR?

Raise awareness about injustice today. One day, start a non-profit.

Journal new ideas today. One day, write a book.

You'll never see amazing impact one day without showing up on day one. The best thing you have going for you is time.

Today can be day one of the rest of your life. Are you ready to change the world?

1
FIGHT

"I could do this all day." —Captain America

Everything fell apart at mile 20. I experienced all the typical side effects of running a marathon—heartbeat racing, accelerated breathing, legs on fire. You know, the fun stuff. Then all of a sudden, *CRACK!*

"How are you doing?" my brother asked.

"My foot hurts," I gasped between breaths.

"This is a marathon. Everything hurts," Andrew responded.

Andrew is my older brother. He had two marathons under his belt compared to my zero. I didn't need his sarcasm. The race was called "Haulin' Aspen" (pun intended) in Bend, Oregon. The course took us through the scenic Deschutes National Forest. The stunning views of pine trees and Mount Bachelor almost made the pain bearable. Almost.

After three hours, we were hitting the wall. The wall is a phenomenon experienced by many endurance athletes. It's when you run out of energy because you're out of glycogen. It feels like you are dying. Runners often say the halfway point in a marathon is mile 20. The idea is that the last 6.2 miles are just as hard as the first 20. I disagree. The last 6.2 are way worse.

I had never run more than 20 miles before that day. I didn't know what would happen exactly. Could I push past the wall? Would I make it to the finish line? How much would I slow down? Every step was uncharted territory. One thing was sure: it would be painful.

The pain in my right foot was different. I had broken it. I could tell it was a stress fracture because I had done the same thing to my left foot back in high school. A stress fracture is an overuse injury caused by repetitive force. Although the crack is tiny, it generates shots of searing pain with every step. Unfortunately, the terrain was much more technical than I expected. Lava rock completely covered some sections of the trail. I foolishly chose to wear my lightweight road shoes instead of my slightly heavier but sturdy trail shoes. Only six miles to go.

"I think I broke my foot," I said.

1. FIGHT

"Really? Can you make it to the finish line?" Andrew asked.

"I don't know," I confessed.

I honestly didn't know if I could finish the race. One day, you will find yourself in this type of situation. You may not be in a literal race, but things will fall apart. Maybe you are dealing with this right now. Maybe you are in the middle of a college degree, and the homework is way more challenging than you thought it would be. Maybe you are a few years into a serious relationship, and now all you do is fight with each other. Maybe you are starting a new job, and the learning curve is entirely overwhelming. When things fall apart, you must face the question: Can you make it to the finish line?

If you want to change the world, you're going to face opposition. Leaders are catalysts for change, and change always creates resistance. Sometimes resistance is embodied in the form of a real human opponent. For whatever reason, someone doesn't want you to win. They could be your competition, they might be jealous, or frankly, they don't like you. These people are resistance incarnate.

YOU'RE GOING TO FACE OPPOSITION.

Other times, resistance takes the form of unforeseen obstacles. A random email complaint that shows up at just the wrong time. A homework assignment which has a back page you didn't see. The materials cost twice as much as your budget. Every project has setbacks, and every hero has a villain. Often, we face a combination of the two.

When resistance comes, what do you do? There are three main options:

First, run away. Avoidance is the most common approach. People generally try to avoid pain, and resistance is painful. There are a lot of different ways to run.

You get a critical email, so you forward it to another team member to respond: #delegation.

A project is close to the deadline, and you won't finish in time. Instead of buckling down and getting things done, you turn in the project late and blame external circumstances.

A co-worker asks you to help them resolve a conflict. You say you'll pray for them and send them on their way.

Whether we pass the problem off, blame shift, or ignore it, none of these tactics help. You can't solve a problem while you are running from it.

Second, give up. Sometimes we surrender. We're tired, so we give way to the resistance. If you can't beat 'em, join 'em.

1. FIGHT

You know the person in the meeting is wrong, but they are louder than you are. So, you don't argue. You go with their idea even though you know it's a bad one.

You face a brutal financial quarter and decide to close up shop.

The education required for your dream career is too challenging/long/expensive, so you go with something more manageable.

Change is not only hard on people; it is hard on the leader. It's always going to be easier to give up, but the best things are always on the other side of difficulty. That's why they call it a *breakthrough*.

Third, fight. There is a third option: we can fight. I'm not talking about getting aggressive. I'm talking about getting resilient. It's more about how many punches you can take than how many you can throw. To fight is to take an honest look at what needs to be done and get to work. Own the critical feedback, deal with the conflict, and speak up. Put in the hours. Stay up late if you have to. Fighting means doing what needs to get done. Leaders who do this aren't overly optimistic about the situation. They know it's going to be hard, but they show up anyway. Yard by yard, they move the ball down the field.

Fight is the ability to keep moving forward regardless of what obstacles come your way. Fight is sailing into a headwind. It's showing up early and staying late. Falling down seven times, getting up eight. You don't have to be intelligent, talented, or even strong to fight. Fight is simple: keep moving forward.

WHATEVER IT TAKES

"But if we do this, who would lead the new church?"
Everyone looked around the room silently.
"I'll do it," I volunteered.

I had no idea what I was signing up for. I was 26 years old—the youngest person in the room by more than a decade. I was sitting in an elder meeting to decide the future of our multi-site church. I wasn't exactly an "elder."

I was at this meeting only because I had recently become a campus pastor. Six months earlier, I had moved out of youth ministry to become the pastor at the second of our two locations. Our church was going through a search process for a lead pastor since the founding pastor resigned. The process was long, and a lot was riding on finding the right person for the job. Three candidates got close, but each time it didn't work out. After two years of waiting for vision and direction, the church grew weary. Slowly, people began to leave. The pastors and elders knew it was time to pivot.

1. FIGHT

The agenda of this meeting was simple: if we don't find a new lead pastor for our multi-site church, then what? Two ideas were on the table. First, we could close down the second location (where I served), consolidate resources, and regroup at the main campus. The other idea was riskier. We could simplify our structure and become two independent churches. After all, these two congregations had been getting by just fine for the past two years. Two medium-sized churches could eliminate many of the complicated systems needed to run a multi-site model. The central campus would keep the same name, logo, branding, etc. The smaller campus (mine) would relaunch as a brand-new church.

The next logical question was, "Who?" Who would do all the work to relaunch a campus as a church? Who would lead this effort? Who even knows how?

In my mind, it was clear. I had been the campus pastor for a whopping six months, so I was the man for the job.

It wasn't that obvious to the rest of the team. I sensed the shock in the room when I volunteered. Everyone got silent. All eyes on me. Next came the objections.

"How would you go about forming a governing board?"

"Have you ever managed a budget this size?"

"Do you know how to get a 501(c)3?"

WHAT ARE YOU WAITING FOR?

"What would your new church name be?"

"What's your vision? Mission? Values? Strategy?"

Like bullets from a gun, the barrage of questions kept coming.

"Listen, I don't know the answers to all these questions right now," I said, "But if I get the opportunity to lead this new church, I promise I'll figure it out. I don't care how hard I have to work or how long it takes, I will see this thing through. Besides, if God is leading us this direction, what could go wrong?" (Actually, a lot could go wrong.)

There was another awkward silence in the room.

"What about you?" an elder gestured to another senior leader in the room. "Where do you see yourself in this potential new structure?"

This leader had twice my theological training and four times my ministry experience. He was a better choice by every metric. But instead of jumping at the opportunity, he brushed it aside.

"I remember when I was in my 20s," the senior leader said. "I had so much fight in me. I believed I could change the world. But I don't think I have it in me to lead something new at this point in my life."

Long story short, I got the job. Not because I was the best choice. Technically speaking, I was the *only* choice. No one else applied. I ended up planting Hill

1. FIGHT

City Church ten months later, in 2018. It was much more challenging than I thought it would be, and I was in way over my head. The thing that got me through that season was the ability to fight. Some people call it grit, perseverance, or hunger. I call it fight. It's when you'll do whatever it takes to get the job done.

Young leaders can have more fight in them because they don't know what they're up against. They are confident because they don't know any better. They live by Han Solo's words, "Never tell me the odds." Fixating on how unlikely the success is won't help you get there. If you're young, you are capable of shocking upsets. Some write it off as beginner's luck, but we know better. Luck has nothing to do with it. A person who's willing to fight will get things done. There is power in having a winning mindset. Pastor Craig Groeschel would agree. "If you think you can't

> **A PERSON WHO'S WILLING TO FIGHT WILL GET THINGS DONE.**

do something, you probably won't. If, on the other hand, you think you can, odds are you will."[2] Older leaders are less likely to fight. Over time, the fight tends to get knocked out of all of us. We've lost too many battles. A big reason we stop fighting is that we're tired. The enemy of fight is fatigue. Many older leaders just don't have the energy anymore (or at least they don't think they do).

WHAT ARE YOU WAITING FOR?

Burnout takes many great leaders out of the game. If you are in the second half of your life, you are probably the most experienced and capable person for the job. Then why might you constantly find yourself on the sidelines? Often, it's not because anyone put you there. You might have chosen the bench because you're tired and it's comfortable. You might be missing the most significant years of impact because you've lost your fight.

DAVID: FEARLESS FIGHTER

One of the best examples of fight comes from the famous story of David and Goliath. Even if you've never picked up a Bible in your life, you probably know the gist. The little guy beats the giant. But there's more to it than that.

The Philistines had come to wage war against the Israelites. They had a secret weapon—Goliath. He was a force to be reckoned with. A giant warrior decked out in the strongest armor. They were so confident in Goliath's military prowess that they were willing to go all-in on their champion.

The challenge was simple. Israel would put forth their best soldier to fight Goliath. Mano a mano. The winner would determine the victory of the battle; the losing nation would become slaves of the winners. Great

1. FIGHT

idea if you are a Philistine. Not so much for Israel. Why? They didn't have any giants.

For forty days, morning and night, Goliath came out and taunted the Israelite army. King Saul and the Israelite army were dismayed and greatly afraid. They had the fight knocked out of them. The soldiers were tired and scared. The odds were not good, and they knew it. King Saul tried to recruit an Israelite champion by offering riches, fame, and even his daughter's hand in marriage. No one stepped forward.

Enter David. He's a scrawny teenage boy. He is the youngest of all his siblings—the runt of the pack. When the rest of his family goes off to war, he is left behind to take care of the sheep. One day he goes down to the front lines to deliver food for his brothers. He hears the taunts from Goliath. David doesn't get it. Why has no one accepted the challenge?

"I'll do it," David volunteers.

King Saul isn't so sure. "You are not able to go against this Philistine to fight with him, for you are but a youth, and he has been a man of war from his youth" (1 Samuel 17:33). Maybe when you're older. Hit the gym; then we'll talk. Grow a beard. Yet David isn't taking "no" for an answer. He knows other candidates aren't exactly lining up, so he lists his resume. "I've protected my sheep from a lion and bear; I can take

Goliath." You've got to credit David with confidence. Killing a fully armed professional soldier is a little more complicated than scaring off wild animals from a flock. David doesn't know that. Even if he did, he doesn't care. His confidence is not mere naïveté; he believes God is with him. "The Lord who delivered me from the paw of the lion and from the paw of the bear will deliver me from the hand of this Philistine" (1 Samuel 17:37). For some reason, Saul agrees to send this kid into battle, and the rest is history. David wins the fight with a well-aimed rock from his slingshot. He gets the money, the fame, and the girl. He goes on to become the King of Israel. David and Goliath is the original underdog story. It amazes and inspires us. And the truth is any of us can learn to fight like David.

LEARNING TO FIGHT

Fighting for a cause. David believed that beating Goliath was of the utmost importance. The stakes were high. He didn't want his whole nation to become Philistine slaves. There is a massive difference between "somebody should do something about that" and "I have to do something." For example, maybe when we see a light bulb that's gone out at our favorite restaurant, we think somebody else should do something about that.

1. FIGHT

We don't have much skin in the game. However, when our own career is on the line, we know we have to do something. When the fight is personal, we'll do whatever it takes to win.

Do you believe what you are doing with your life matters? Many people do mediocre work because they think what they are doing has little meaning. Those who think they are living out their calling give it everything they've got. If you want a cause worth fighting for, you need a cause that's bigger than yourself. Motivation crumbles if a job is just another way to pay the bills. In whatever you do, look for the people. You might not need to change careers or switch degree programs to get your fight back. Shift your mindset to see how what you are currently doing helps people.

Maybe you're already in your sweet spot. Run with it. If you've lost your purpose somewhere along the way, remember what got you into your line of work in the first place. How are you helping? If you wrestle about that question for a week and honestly can't come up with an answer, maybe a career change is a good option. Life is too short to live for ourselves. Once you are in touch with your calling, you have a cause worth fighting for. It'll allow you to endure more than you can imagine. You'll get up early and stay up late because what you are doing is about more than yourself.

WHAT ARE YOU WAITING FOR?

Rhythm of rest. The Israelite soldiers on the front lines were exhausted, short on supplies, and humiliated from Goliath's constant taunting. The senior leader in that elder meeting was tired from years of ministry. If fatigue is the great enemy of a fight, rest prepares us for it. David was itching to see some action. He had been at home watching sheep. When he brought his brothers food, he was looking for an opportunity to get involved. Kind of like David, I was an eager 26-year-old who couldn't wait to make a difference. We have to be resting well enough to have the energy to fight when it matters most. If we're all fight and no rest, it's only a matter of time until we burn out.

A saying I live by is, "Work hard, rest hard." Both are incredibly important. I take the work I do seriously. Some seasons are busier than others. The season I'm in right now involves a $500K fundraising campaign, a building renovation on a 110-year-old building, and a church merger. All of this is on top of regular ministry duties and navigating the major cultural shifts in the post-COVID world. Somehow every week, to my surprise, I get everything done.

I work hard because I believe what I'm doing matters. I hope that people will experience renewal and revival when our church is on track. I get the opportunity to tell people that God loves them and wants to give them

1. FIGHT

abundant life. Pastors have one of the more naturally fulfilling jobs out there. However, pastors are also notorious for burnout. I talk to church leaders all the time, and I can tell you that many of them are both physically and emotionally exhausted. Even though the ministry dropout rate seems to be slowing down, still 33% of American pastors seriously considered quitting in the last year.[3] I also take rest very seriously. I choose not to bring work home with me so that I can be present with my family. I have screen time limits on my phone, so I'm not distracting my soul into oblivion. I practice Sabbath rest every Friday night to Saturday night. The Sabbath is just as much about what you do as what you don't do. It's a day to connect with God, with yourself, and with others. Rest hard. Don't live every day like it's a fight—it's not. Don't waste your energy boxing the air so that you have nothing left when Goliath shows up. Consistently commit to a rhythm of refreshment so that you're ready for the fight of your life. Many people talk about a work/life balance. They should be talking about a work/rest balance. Work and rest in a proper ratio make a balance, and the best leaders figure this out.

Confidence beyond yourself. It wasn't David's confidence in himself that made him go toe-to-toe with Goliath. He didn't overestimate his strength. Fight isn't about thinking you're bigger or better than you are. And

WHAT ARE YOU WAITING FOR?

David didn't underestimate Goliath. We'll never win by pretending our problems aren't real. Rather, David had confidence beyond himself. He knew that God was with him, and that changed the equation. There comes a breaking point where the opposition we face is truly more than we can take. In moments like these, our strength has to come from somewhere outside of ourselves.

> **OUR STRENGTH HAS TO COME FROM SOMEWHERE OUTSIDE OF OURSELVES.**

You are the resident expert on your weaknesses. If you're paying attention, nobody knows your failures better than you. When resistance rises in your life, the voices in your head will start going off like alarm bells. Every insecurity will rise to the surface, and you'll want to run away or give up.

"You can't do this."

"Just quit."

"Get a real job."

"You're not _____ enough." Fill in the blank.

In times like these, we need more than our willpower to fight. Stop calculating the odds. Instead of focusing on what you don't have, take an inventory of what you *do* have. David had five smooth stones and a slingshot. Your confidence might come from great teammates, technology, resources, or strategy. I've found that the

1. FIGHT

only unshakeable foundation that can hold the total weight of my problems is Jesus. Prayer is the fuel that keeps me moving forward. "What then shall we say to these things? If God is for us, who can be against us?" (Romans 8:31). If he's not already, Jesus can be the foundation you depend on when storms come your way.

LEVERAGE YOUR FIGHT

Stand firm. Once you've got your fight back, you've got to use it to your advantage. In challenging seasons, this looks a lot like rafting through the rapids. You'll need all the strength you can muster to hold on for dear life.

Your task list seems unending. It's not.

No one sees things your way in the meetings. If you're speaking wisdom, they'll eventually come around.

The training phase is far from over. One day you'll be done.

The doors of opportunity that are opening for all your friends keep slamming in your face. Keep knocking.

Your income stream is drying up. Pivot and find a new path forward.

Sometimes our ability to fight is the only thing keeping us going. Smooth sailing is on the other side of the whitewater. It might be a fight, but it's worth it.

WHAT ARE YOU WAITING FOR?

The season leading up to planting Hill City Church was a lot like hanging on for dear life. I didn't know if we would have enough money to pay the bills after the first month. I've never had so many things on a to-do list that I had no idea how to do. By the time I finally checked off one task, there were two more to replace it—one step forward, two steps back.

Miraculously, I didn't give up. I was able to come home each night knowing that tomorrow was a new day. That season was not only challenging but exciting. I remember when we finally got the new building sign installed. Then we had our first church service. We weren't just paying the bills—we started talking about our next hire. The vision was becoming real. Remember, whatever hardship you go through is only a season. The sun will rise again. There are good things prepared for those who stand firm.

Move forward. The ability to fight doesn't just come in handy during difficult seasons. In normal times, the ability to fight is the difference between the employee who goes the extra mile and the one who counts down the minutes until 5 o'clock. Leadership guru Patrick Lencioni describes these extra-mile people as "hungry." "Hungry people are always looking for more. More things to do. More to learn. More responsibility to take on. Hungry people almost never have to be pushed by a

1. FIGHT

manager to work harder because they are self-motivated and diligent."[4]

When I was 18, I worked at a carpet warehouse one summer. I got to drive a forklift with an attachment called "the stinger." It was a ten-foot pole that tapered to a pointed end. On my first day, my boss showed me a YouTube compilation video of epic forklift fails. Then he handed me the keys and said, "Try not to crash."

The end of my first workday came, and I hadn't finished with my project. I was right in the middle of changing out all the rugs in the showroom. The following day I showed up on time, clocked in, and resumed hanging mats. My boss was shocked to see me already working when he rolled in 15 minutes late. I thought it was normal. He acted like I had just solved world peace.

"Who told you to do the rugs?" he questioned.

"You did. Yesterday," I answered.

"We need more people like you around here, kid."

I worked hard at that carpet warehouse all summer. Every morning, I prayed on the bike ride to work that God would use me as a light to my co-workers. The last week before I went off to college, my boss asked me what was different about me. I was able to share my faith with him that day. I explained that I wasn't just working for him; I was working for Jesus.

WHAT ARE YOU WAITING FOR?

Pick your fight. Practice fighting in the small ways, and you'll be ready when serious battles come your way. David practiced with his slingshot while he looked after sheep. When the lion came around, he was ready. David didn't stop there. He kept practicing. Next came a bear that didn't stand a chance. He kept practicing. The road led him to Goliath. Faithfulness in small jobs leads to big opportunities. Hone your skills now, so you'll be ready for later.

One day, an opportunity will come your way. It will likely appear just out of reach. Maybe your dream college is enrolling, but you're not sure your GPA is high enough. Or maybe a great company is hiring, but you are way under-qualified. You have the chance to date the guy/girl of your dreams, but they are out of your league. Now we are talking. In these moments, stop looking at the "but's" and step up to the plate. The best ambitions are the hardest ones to achieve. There comes a point where you need to stop calculating the odds and fight for your dreams. You won't get there in a day, a week, or maybe even a year. But one day, if you keep moving forward, you'll reach the finish line.

Back to the marathon story. I kept running. Getting through those last 6.2 miles turned out to be one of the most demanding physical challenges I've ever faced. Miles 22 to 24 felt like they were straight uphill. Our

1. FIGHT

pace slowed down significantly in the last segment. It wasn't pretty, but we kept moving. That's what *fight* is all about.

Running a marathon was on my bucket list. I had trained for that race six days a week for four months straight. I paid the $75 registration fee. (Why do races cost so much money, anyway?) I drove five hours from Boise to Bend. My wife and daughter were waiting for me. Getting through those last miles, I didn't care if my foot fell off; I was going to finish the race. After I crossed the finish line, I collapsed to the ground and wept.

You can fight, too. Whatever opposition you face, just keep moving. The sweetest victories come from the most brutal battles. If you keep going, inch by inch, you'll get to the finish line. Fight for a cause that matters and change the world.

THINK ABOUT IT

Growth takes time. Before you move on, slow down long enough to reflect, journal, or discuss these questions:

1. When was a time that you weren't sure if you could make it to the finish line (literal or metaphorical)? How did it turn out?

WHAT ARE YOU WAITING FOR?

2. Do you naturally tend to run away, give up, or fight when you encounter difficult situations? Why do you think that is?
3. Why do you think David stepped onto the battlefield when no one else did? What would give you the same courage as David?
4. On a scale of 1 to 10, how well-rested are you today? What adjustments do you need to make so that you can be regularly refreshed?
5. Think of a battle you are facing right now. Is the cause worth fighting for? Where does your confidence come from? What will help you stay in the fight?
6. What are the little things you can be faithful in today that will lead to major opportunities in the future?

2
POSSIBILITY

"Impossible is not a fact. It's an opinion. Impossible is potential. Impossible is temporary. Impossible is nothing."
—*Muhammad Ali*

On March 5, 2019, I prayed one of the biggest prayers I've ever prayed. It was one of those shot-in-the-dark prayers. I know the exact date because Jake wrote it down.

Jake is one of my best friends, a co-worker, and the Associate Pastor of Hill City Church. We went to college together. We were in each other's weddings. There's still a picture floating around on the internet of me with dreadlocks as one of his groomsmen. I got a haircut the following week. His wife will never let me live it down.

WHAT ARE YOU WAITING FOR?

He's also a young leader. We were both 27 years old when we launched Hill City Church together back in 2018. When people asked us if they could meet one of the pastors, we would say, "You're looking at them."

In March of 2019, we were beginning to scope out long-term options for a meeting location for our church. When we launched Hill City, we took on the remaining lease term for a commercial property that used to be a grocery store. The monthly cost of the lease was more than half our budget. While we were blessed to have a ready-to-go meeting location from the start, we knew that we'd need to figure out a permanent solution one day.

We were meeting with another pastor who led a church in downtown Boise. The church was named Capitol City Christian Church. The building was initially built by First Christian Church in Boise back in 1910. It's a beautifully designed historic church building. It has stained glass windows, balcony seating, and a massive dome in the ceiling that creates impressive acoustics.

The cherry on top is the location. Real estate in downtown Boise is tough to come by. Yet that part of town is ideal for reaching Boise State University, the high school, and the North End neighborhoods. The purpose of this meeting was to explore what it could look like

2. POSSIBILITY

to rent from Capitol City. Who knew where it might go from there?

By the end of the meeting, it was clear this pastor was tired. The numbers of church members were diminishing, and he was having a difficult time leading the kind of change that needed to occur. Numerous building issues required attention, but the funding was not available to fix them. He said they would be happy to rent an evening time slot to us for $500 a month. This monthly rate was a steal compared to what we were paying at the time in our North End building 1.8 miles away. We were still about a year and a half from the end of our lease, so we thanked him for his time and told him we'd keep the option in mind.

As Jake and I walked out of the meeting, we had a sudden urge to pray. We began walking through the neighborhoods surrounding the church and praying. As we walked, we saw high school kids playing sports. We began to dream as we walked by dozens of mid-century houses. If we looked through the trees, we could see the Boise capitol building popping up a block away.

WE HAD A SUDDEN URGE TO PRAY.

We prayed a blessing over the dwindling congregation, hoping the best for the people. We prayed that God would establish our six-month-old church plant by leading us to the right building. Then came the biggest prayer I'd ever prayed. Authors Jim Collins and Jerry Porras talk about the idea of a "Big Hairy Audacious Goal."[5] This was our Big Hairy Audacious Prayer. To be honest, I'm not sure who prayed it first, Jake or me. All I know is that we both prayed for the same thing that afternoon: "God, would you give us *this* church building?"

We didn't know how or when, but we asked God for it anyway. The most plausible scenario would be for the aging congregation to move to a smaller building and sell their building to us (hopefully for a deal). We didn't specify. Surely God would sort out the details.

A year went by, and nothing changed. Then in March 2020, COVID-19 came to Idaho. Unbeknownst to us, the lead pastor of Capitol City Christian Church had already accepted a job offer in another state and was on his way out. COVID was hard for every church but especially difficult for congregations that didn't have an online presence. When you add a major leadership transition, it was clear that Capitol City needed some kind of directional change.

I started praying for Capitol City consistently during this time. I reached out to David, one of the church members, and asked if there was any way we could help. He said they were getting by alright, but he'd let me

2. POSSIBILITY

know. I kept praying. The wheels were turning. Could this lead to something? Would God bring good out of this challenging season? Was this the answer to our Big Hairy Audacious Prayer?

Three more months went by. Silence this whole time. I was busy figuring out how to lead through COVID. I had also begun negotiating the contract for a new five-year lease term at our current building. Yes, it was expensive, but at least it was stable. Whenever COVID ended, we wanted to make sure we had a facility to come back to.

Then in the first week of July 2020, everything came to a head. I had an increasing sense of angst about staying at our current location. We had paid tens of thousands of dollars for an empty building over the last few months. Not only that, but our church was growing while exclusively online. In our Monday staff meeting, we started to brainstorm other options. Some were a little out of the ordinary. What if we didn't have a building but stayed online after COVID? What if we switched to a house church model? What if we went portable and met in a high school? No idea was off-limits. It was a proper brainstorming session where anything was on the table.

That Tuesday night, we had an elder meeting in my backyard. It would be our final meeting to finalize the

WHAT ARE YOU WAITING FOR?

details of our lease and vote to sign it. All the crazy ideas from Monday's staff meeting were going to change the agenda a little bit.

The day beforehand, I had gotten a text. It was David from Capitol City. He asked if I could meet Tuesday morning. As we met for coffee, David explained that he had been consulting with the Capitol City elders. They were evaluating their options for how to move forward in light of not having a lead pastor. They concluded that their best option was to pursue a merger with another vibrant church aligned closely with their mission. Capitol City had been in conversations with another church, but it didn't look like it would work out. David asked if Hill City Church would consider merging with Capitol City Christian Church.

At one point, he said, "We don't have much to offer, except a paid-off building in downtown Boise."

This news was going to change the agenda even more. I brought ice cream sandwiches that night. The team started the meeting thinking we were finalizing a commercial lease, and by the end, we were committed to exploring a church merger with Capitol City. Everyone necessary approved the merger by October, and our two churches joined together in January 2021. Big prayer. Bigger God.

2. POSSIBILITY

Not everyone prays big prayers. Not everyone sets Big Hairy Audacious Goals. Those that do find themselves experiencing a lot more "coincidences" than those that don't.

If you want to change the world, you need a trait called *possibility*. It is the belief that anything is possible. Young people are more likely to have it because the world hasn't chewed them up yet. Older leaders tend to be more pessimistic because they've faced the real world. All of us can possess possibility because, ultimately, it's a choice.

A University of Michigan summer leadership course teaches students, "Have a healthy disregard for the impossible."[6] That's what I'm talking about! Possibility is the decision to believe that God can do the impossible.

KIDS GET IT

Do you remember when you were a kid? Go back further than high school or junior high. What was your life like when you were ten years old? More specifically, what games did you play? If you were anything like me, you played all kinds of games that existed entirely in your imagination. My brother and I would run through the woods with sticks pretending to be knights of the round table. The next day we were explorers in outer space.

WHAT ARE YOU WAITING FOR?

Odds are, you played games of imagination too. You had an easy bake oven and pretended you were a world-renowned chef. You had sidewalk chalk, and you created masterpieces that could rival Van Gogh's *Starry Night*. You talked to dolls or action figures (I'll admit that I collected Beanie Babies). Kids have tremendous imaginations, and imagination is at the heart of possibility.

Once I had the opportunity to speak at a youth camp in Australia. I wanted to get to know some of the campers a bit better, so I asked a young girl what she wanted to be when she grew up. I expected her to say that she wanted to be a hairstylist. For a 10-year-old, she was already great at it. All weekend, teenagers were asking her to do their hair. She knew how to do every braid in the book. If that's what she can do at 10, imagine how great she would be with another decade of experience. It's just practical. But her answer to the question was not a hairstylist. Do you want to know what she said?

"I'm going to be a famous singer."

Not, I *want* to be a famous singer. I'm *going* to be a famous singer. She is confident because she still has enough imagination to believe in possibility. She's not concerned with how practical her career choice is. One day she might sing a hit that reaches the top

2. POSSIBILITY

of the charts. Even if she doesn't, at least she has the imagination required to dream. And she doesn't just believe; she practices. Hope leads to action. The last night of camp, I watched as she stood up before the rest of the campers, all of them older than she, and sang a solo. When was the last time you sang a solo before a crowd? Possibility is powerful.

When I was a kid, my career of choice was a ninja. I think I watched a little too much *Mighty Morphin Power Rangers*. As I got older, I picked a more logical choice: a comic book artist. Who wouldn't want to draw pictures of Batman all day? I even job-shadowed a cartoonist from the local newspaper my senior year of high school. I believed I could make a career out of drawing cartoons. It was possible, and I was pursuing it.

Before my senior year of high school ended, I had settled on a more reasonable career. I would get an engineering degree from the University of Alaska Fairbanks. Then I would get my teaching certificate and become a high school math teacher. Wait a minute; what happened? A math teacher is light-years away from ninja or comic artist.

My career choice shifted because I traded possible for practical. I was good at math. I had scholarships to a local university. The real-world set in, and I stopped dreaming. *Possible* is captivated with what could be.

Practical is consumed by what makes the most sense on paper. The problem is, no one ever changed the world by doing what already made the most sense on paper.

YOU GREW UP, TOO

I don't know when it happened, but I'm guessing that you grew up, too. You traded *possible* for *practical*. Maybe you realized your dream job didn't pay very well, so you settled for something safe with a salary. Or maybe you got into your desired line of work, but it wasn't all you hoped it would be. People can be mean, and failure happens to all of us. The world has a way of chewing up bright-eyed kids and spitting out boring adults. Along the way, we become pessimists instead of dreamers.

> **WE BECOME PESSIMISTS INSTEAD OF DREAMERS.**

Pastor Carey Nieuwhof says it like this: "Most cynics are former optimists. You'd never know it now, but there was a time when they were hopeful, enthusiastic, and even cheerful. There's something inside the human spirit that wants to hope, wants to think things will get better. Nearly everyone starts life with a positive outlook."[7]

A few years ago, I started seeing a counselor. I remember talking to him about my new boss during a session. My counselor asked me what I thought about

2. POSSIBILITY

him, and I had to admit I wasn't so sure. "I guess I'm just a naturally skeptical person," I said.

Before I continued, he stopped me by asking, "What do you mean?"

"Well, I guess I've always had a hard time trusting people. When I meet someone new, especially someone whom I'm going to work with, I usually view that person with suspicion."

Then my counselor did some counseling. "Josh, no one is born suspicious or cynical. If you have a hard time trusting people, it's because somebody has broken your trust in the past. Can you think of anyone that has betrayed your trust?"

This insight shook me. I thought that cynicism was just part of my personality type. Maybe you've done the same thing. You've been pretending that you are just a negative person. Were you pessimistic as a three-year-old?

That day with the counselor I started a journey inward to find out what moments had shaped me into an unbeliever. I've had to unlearn some of the lessons of adulthood so that I could regain my childlike imagination. You can do this, too.

WHAT ARE YOU WAITING FOR?

MARY: IMPOSSIBLE MOTHER

If you were God and wanted to come into the world, how would you do it? I'd make a scene for sure—parting the clouds, thunder and lightning, the whole nine yards. Maybe I'd play some 80's rock music. "Rock You Like a Hurricane" should get everyone's attention.

It's a good thing I'm not God.

Two thousand years ago, God chose to come to earth in the most unexpected way—ordinarily. There was no red carpet or press conference, just a few shepherds showing up at the barn to see little baby Jesus asleep on the hay. One of the most intriguing details of the nativity story is that God got to pick his mother. We make millions of decisions throughout our lives, but none of us decides our parents. God could have chosen for Jesus to be born to any woman. Whom did he choose? A twelve-year-old peasant girl.

There are many theories as to why God chose Mary. Maybe she was devout and holy. Perhaps it was to exalt someone who came from a humble situation. Maybe God knew she would raise Jesus in the wisdom and instruction of the Lord. There's probably truth to all these points. I think God chose Mary because she believed God could do the impossible.

2. POSSIBILITY

If you read the nativity story in Luke 1, you'll notice a contrast between Mary, the mother of Jesus, and Zechariah, the father of John (the Baptist). Mary and Zechariah both received good news from God but responded in two different ways.

Unlike Mary, Zechariah was old. He and his wife Elizabeth had no children. They had tried their whole marriage but couldn't get pregnant. Heartbroken, they kept praying that God would bless them with a child. One day, Zechariah was serving at the temple in Jerusalem.

He was a priest, and it was his turn to burn incense in the holy place. Entering the holy place was a sacred job done by only one priest at a time. Zechariah quietly entered the small room, fully expecting to be alone. To his surprise, he turned around and saw the angel Gabriel standing behind him. Imagine the jump scare!

But the angel said to him, "Do not be afraid, Zechariah, for your prayer has been heard, and your wife Elizabeth will bear you a son, and you shall call his name John" (Luke 1:13). Did you catch that? *Your prayer has been heard.* It may take decades for an answer, but God is listening to us the whole time. Look at Zechariah's response: "And Zechariah said to the angel, 'How shall I know this? For I am an old man, and my wife is advanced in years.'" (Luke 1:18). Instead of gratitude, Zechariah wanted proof. Sure, he had prayed for a child, but along the way he had grown to no longer expect God to do anything about it. Now that God was moving, he wasn't buying it. *Prove it.*

Gabriel seems annoyed. He came all the way from the heavenly realms to deliver this message. First of all, Gabriel points out the obvious. "You want proof? I'm an angel!" Then he dishes out a consequence for Zechariah's unbelief.

He would be unable to speak until the baby was born.

Zechariah and Elizabeth still got their blessing. Once John was born, Zechariah was able to speak again. But for nine months, he had the "opportunity" to reflect on the power of God silently.

In the meantime, Gabriel appeared to Mary. He told her that God had picked her to give birth to the Son of the Most High. She wasn't praying for this. Mary wasn't looking for a miracle. Humbly, she responded by asking how this was possible since she's a virgin. God had opened wombs of the infertile before, but immaculate conception was impossible. Her question is more curiosity than doubt.

Gabriel explained that this baby would be born by the Holy Spirit and the power of God. Then he closed by saying, "For nothing will be impossible with

2. POSSIBILITY

God" (Luke 1:37). That's all it took for Mary. She responded, "Behold, I am the servant of the Lord; let it be to me according to your word" (Luke 1:38). The rest is history—literally. Mary gave birth to the Savior of the world. She believed that nothing is impossible for God. Her faith made Mary the perfect candidate to raise Jesus Christ. She said yes to this calling, no matter how impossible it was. Possibility unlocks the door to participating in the unlikely and experiencing the miraculous.

Thankfully, even if we've lost our sense of wonder over time, we can get it back.

LEARNING POSSIBILITY

Take time to dream. Kids are dreamers. My wife and I have creative kids. Let me tell you, they come up with some crazy ideas! One moment my daughter is pretending she's a princess, and the next, she's a dragon. Children don't have to try to use their imagination. It's their default operating mode. However, as we grow older, we become more concerned with the way things currently are than how they could be.

Bob Goff explains it like this, "Our dreams are birthed in childlike innocence, but as we grow up, we discover more information that can be a buzzkill to our ambitions."[8] We have too much information and not enough dreams. If we want to rediscover a sense of possibility, we have to schedule times to dream. If you work on a team, you can do this by having an actual brainstorming session. I say "actual brainstorming session" because we've probably all been in meetings where they say, "no idea is a bad idea."

Then moments later, everyone is laughing you out of the room or shooting down your thoughts with a machine gun of "what-abouts." What about this? What about that? Brainstorming is only valuable when everyone can share their ideas uninhibited. The ideas that come up in a meeting like this may not end up being the finished product. But you'll be a whole lot closer to the finish line than if you simply talked about all the ways that your project could fail.

We also need to take time to dream by ourselves and with our families. Every January, my wife and I go on a special date to discuss our dreams for the new year. I've found this to be much more helpful than the typical New Year resolutions. We share our goals and how we can support one another on our journey.

Dreaming on my own looks a lot more like quiet time. You can't dream about the future when your mind is preoccupied with the noise of the present. Set down your phone and pick up a journal. Ask yourself the

2. POSSIBILITY

question, "If I could be doing anything five years from now, what would it be?" That's the question that initially got me thinking about finding a more permanent church home.

I knew it wasn't realistic for our church to own a building in five years, but I entertained the idea anyway. I thought about the location, size, and specifications. Long before I prayed the crazy prayer for God to give us a building, the ideal facility already existed in my mind. Instead of waiting five or ten years to purchase land and build a building, God gave us a home in a little over one year.

Pray big. Prayer is the fuel that feeds the fire of possibility. When we think only of our power and resources, our dreams fall flat. But when we speak to the omnipotent God of the universe, our imaginations begin to run wild. It's like the moment where Jesus asks the blind beggar Bartimaeus, "What do you want me to do for you?" (Mark 10:51). Bartimaeus could have said anything. "Do you have five bucks? How about you buy lunch?" Instead, he asked Jesus to do the impossible. "Make me see." Jesus did it. We need to spend time praying that God would do the impossible.

> **PRAYER IS THE FUEL THAT FEEDS THE FIRE OF POSSIBILITY.**

WHAT ARE YOU WAITING FOR?

Mark Batterson challenges us to pray bigger and bolder prayers: "Bold prayers honor God, and God honors bold prayers. God isn't offended by your biggest dreams or boldest prayers. He is offended by anything less. If your prayers aren't impossible to you, they are insulting to God."[9]

Small prayers get trivial answers. Impossible prayers get miracles. I don't know about you, but I want to see miracles in my life. I don't just pray for an average marriage. I pray that God would give me the best marriage on the planet. I don't just pray that my kids would be "nice" and get good grades. I pray that they would change the world in more fantastic ways than I do. I don't just pray for church growth. I pray for renewal and revival in our time. Every time you see God do something unique, you will grow in the belief that nothing will be impossible for God.

Tomorrow is a new day. The reason we become cynical as we get older isn't simply due to age. It's because older people carry around more pain. More time in this broken world usually translates to more brokenness in our lives. We have all experienced hurt, failure, and loss. You probably didn't choose the negative baggage that you picked up along the way. What few people realize is that you can select what baggage you bring with you each day.

2. POSSIBILITY

You might have a hard time with people because of a person who hurt you. Maybe a close friend betrayed your trust, or a boss made your life miserable for years. Maybe you have a father wound. The pain of these situations is valid. If the damage is severe, seeing a counselor would be wise. Just because that person took something from you in the past doesn't mean you have to let them rob you of your future.

The only way I know how to break free is to forgive. Forgiveness doesn't mean minimizing the pain or pretending it didn't happen. It also doesn't mean forgetting. Forgiveness means choosing to cancel the debt. You acknowledge what the other person owes you. Then you simply decide not to make them pay up. If you've experienced grace from God, you can now extend that grace to someone else. If you're a Christian, you can also rest easy knowing that you are not the ultimate judge. You can let someone off your hook because you know they are on God's. Sometimes forgiveness leads to the reconciliation of the relationship, and sometimes it doesn't. Either way, forgiveness is the key to opening the prison door. Only after we open that door do we realize that we were the ones trapped the whole time.

Remember that God's mercies are new every morning. If you have a hard heart, let God soften it day by day. Set your alarm clock early so that you can see the sunrise each morning. As you sip your coffee and look at the sun, remember that today is brimming with possibility. There is no problem too big for God to solve. There is no pain too deep for God to heal. I challenge you to do this for a month and watch how your perspective changes.

LEVERAGING POSSIBILITY

Take risks. The first way to leverage possibility is to take risks. No one ever changed the world by playing it safe. Stop worrying about what could go wrong if your idea fails. Start dreaming about what could go right if it works. Longtime Disney CEO Bob Iger lives by the leadership principle, "Status quo is a losing strategy."[10] During Bob's fifteen-year run as CEO, he broadened Disney's intellectual property by acquiring Pixar, Marvel Entertainment, Lucasfilm, and 21st Century Fox. Each of these was a multi-billion-dollar purchase. Now that's a risk. However, Bob saw the value through the cost. Not only did each of these purchases offer a gold mine of creative potential, but each would be pillars to the success of launching Disney+, which couldn't have come at a better time to meet the at-home entrainment market created by COVID-19. Big risks, big reward.

2. POSSIBILITY

You should be taking risks too. Maybe not multi-billion-dollar purchases, but you get the idea. The most dangerous person on the battlefield is the one who has nothing left to lose. The problem with some of us is that we have gotten so comfortable with where we currently are. We don't want to do something different if it risks losing what we've got. The problem with this thinking is that what got you where you are now likely won't get you where you are going.

The world is changing faster than ever. If we refuse to change, our context and competition will outpace us. Not that we should bet the farm every time. We should take calculated risks. The point is that we must embrace possibility if we want to see change. The future belongs to those who believe enough to experiment and try new things.

Aim high. Possibility allows you to set your standards higher. That ten-year-old girl at camp didn't just want to be a singer. She wanted to be a *famous* singer. Mary woke up every day knowing she wasn't just raising a child. She was raising the Son of the Most High God. Your mindset makes a difference. Some of us set our standards low so that we aren't let down. I can't be disappointed if I wasn't expecting much, right? You may not be disappointed, but you also won't make much of a difference. You get to decide.

WHAT ARE YOU WAITING FOR?

Allow yourself to imagine what could be. I've never written a book before. When I was organizing the notes for it on my computer, I titled the folder "Books" instead of "Book." Who knows if I'll ever write another book? But I might as well aim high. The difference between an optimist and a pessimist isn't that optimists simply have better outcomes, but that optimists try more times. Stop giving up on your dreams before you've even had them.

Scott Harrison didn't just want to build a well and provide clean water to a village. He wanted to bring clean and safe water to every person on the planet.[11] So far, his mission "Charity: Water" has helped over 12 million people. Even if he doesn't solve the entire water crisis in his lifetime, Scott's life's work will still be an incredible success. But here's the thing—he might just see his Big Hairy Audacious Goal completed. He would never have gotten this far without a youthful belief in possibility.

Think about your goals. Are they audacious or safe? What about your prayers? Are they practical or impossible? Take time right now to dream bigger dreams. Shoot for the moon, and don't hold back. Come up with a life vision that scares you a little bit. That's when you'll know you are on the right track. Each day, work at it, bit by bit. Chip away at the critics instead of letting them

2. POSSIBILITY

chip away at you. If you keep believing in possibility long enough, you'll see the impossible become a reality.

THINK ABOUT IT

Growth takes time. Before you move on, slow down long enough to reflect, journal, or discuss these questions:

1. What's the biggest goal you've ever made? What's the craziest prayer you've ever prayed?
2. Think back to when you were ten years old. What did you want to be when you grew up? Do you still have the same dream?
3. What are the practical considerations that crowd out your imagination?
4. Why do you think Mary was open to accept Gabriel's news, while Zechariah was more unreceptive? Which one do you relate to more?
5. When do you take time to dream about your future? What kind of environment helps fuel your imagination (e.g., what kind of people, places, and things)?
6. What would you do if you knew you couldn't fail? What's stopping you from doing it?

WHAT ARE YOU WAITING FOR?

7. What are some calculated risks you need to take today so that you can get where you are going tomorrow?
8. What is your crazy prayer that you will keep praying?

3
WEAKNESS

"Why don't I tell you what my greatest weaknesses are? I work too hard, I care too much, and sometimes I can be too invested in my job." —Michael Scott, The Office

My first car was a 1998 Subaru Legacy. Before getting the car, I had been able to bike everywhere I went. Neither snow nor rain nor heat would keep me from where I was going. Then everything changed when I got a girlfriend.

I started dating Shaina (now my wife) at the end of my junior year in college. I figured out quickly that it's a whole lot harder to take a girl out when you don't have a car. There are only so many dates within walking distance. I was always asking friends in a pinch if I could borrow their vehicles—only to find an empty tank of gas.

WHAT ARE YOU WAITING FOR?

The day that convinced me to buy a vehicle was when I borrowed my boss's car and accidentally backed it up into a large landscaping rock. (Who puts a boulder on the side of the driveway?) Five hundred dollars later, I figured it was time to look for something of my own.

The Subaru seemed like a dream come true. I knew the previous owner, and he gave me a good deal. The engine ran, the radio worked, and the heater blew hot air. That was enough for me. Soon I would learn the truth about why cheap cars are so cheap. This lesson couldn't have come at a worse time.

On Christmas Eve, I had planned an elaborate scavenger hunt for Shaina all around town. We would drive throughout Boise looking for clues with little presents interspersed along the way. The quest would eventually lead us to a Christmas tree next to the picnic table, where I had asked Shaina out for the first time. The final gift? An engagement ring.

Long story short, she said yes! We got back into the car to drive over to a friend's Christmas party to celebrate. Moments after we pulled out of the parking lot, the lights on the dashboard began flashing on and off. Next, the radio shut off, and the power steering went out. Panicking, I pulled over to the side of the road and shut off the engine. After a few minutes, I turned the keys in the ignition to start it up again—nothing.

3. WEAKNESS

I looked over at Shaina, "You still want to marry me?"

Over the coming months, I discovered there was a problem deep within the car's electric system. It kept burning up the alternator. I asked the mechanic what it would take to fix the car, and he told me it wasn't worth it. The cost to find and fix the problem was more than the car's value. My solution? YouTube.

Every time the alternator died, I would remove it while watching a step-by-step video on my phone. Then I would pop it in my backpack, ride my bike down to the automotive shop, and exchange it for a new one. I did this a half dozen times. I may not be a mechanic, but I can change an alternator.

Each time I replaced the part, the car would work for a handful of months until it started acting up again. I was only ever able to *manage* the problem, never solve it completely. This whole mystery electric problem earned my Subaru a new name: the "White Witch." She always managed to break down at the worst times. Not only did she act up during our engagement, but she died in the hotel parking lot on our wedding day!

I distinctly remember another time the car broke down. Shaina and I were married and living in a small apartment. She was working part-time and going to school. I was crazy busy at work. Our schedules were jam-packed, and it was a delicate balance sharing our

WHAT ARE YOU WAITING FOR?

one car. This particular evening, we were having our friend Tony over for dinner. We were low on groceries, so I hopped in the car to make a quick run to the store. When I turned the ignition, nothing happened. *The White Witch strikes again!*

I called Tony to cancel our plans.

"Hey bro, I'm sorry we can't do dinner tonight," I said, embarrassed.

"Oh bummer! Why not?" Tony questioned.

"The car is dead again and we're out of food at the apartment. I've got to fix the car so we can get around this week," I vented. He could sense the frustration in my voice.

"You take the alternator out and I'll come pick you up," Tony offered. By this point, all my friends knew the tricks of the White Witch.

"Don't worry about it," I protested.

"See you soon," Tony ended. He hung up before I could get another word in.

That evening wasn't what I was expecting—it was better. Tony drove me to the automotive shop to trade out my broken alternator. Then he took me out for pizza at my favorite place. Instead of hosting my friend, he was buying me dinner. Fixing the car could wait. As we sat down to eat, I shared all the stressful things that had been happening in my life. Driving around a ticking

3. WEAKNESS

time bomb of a car was making my life miserable. After I finished talking, Tony said a line that will always stick with me.

"It's okay to ask for help."

ALL BY MYSELF

Most of us wait way too long before asking for help. We get to the breaking point before we tell someone that we are struggling. The more successful we become, the less we depend on other people. From a young age, our parents celebrate us for doing something "all by yourself." Maybe we should also be teaching our kids it's okay to ask for help.

> **IT'S OKAY TO ASK FOR HELP.**

Independence is a cultural value in America. We have a Declaration of Independence and an Independence Day. We celebrate stories of men and women who trailblazed and climbed their way to the top. Even if you don't live in America, you've probably seen these stories told in movies. American success stories like Ray Kroc of McDonald's, Steve Jobs of Apple Inc., and Mark Zuckerberg of Facebook have all become major motion pictures. Each of these characters represents the typical self-made man.

WHAT ARE YOU WAITING FOR?

It reminds me of the game King of the Hill. Did you ever play that as a kid? I grew up in Fairbanks, Alaska, so we had plenty of snow mounds from freshly plowed parking lots. The rules of King of the Hill are simple: get on top and stay on top. Of course, everyone else is also trying to get to the top of the hard-as-concrete snow pile. There is lots of pushing and shoving. King of the Hill is great if you are big. It's a game that relies upon strength. It's not as fun if you are small and weak. The game often ended with some poor kid falling too hard and bursting into tears. Usually, this was me.

Most of us develop an all-by-myself attitude over time. We try to live life on our own. We don't ask for help, or we feel bad if we do. The times that we let our guard down and share with vulnerability are few and far between. Even if we somehow make it to the top, we discover that life is lonely on top of the hill. There can only be one king, and it's not supposed to be you.

Young people today are often more open about their weaknesses than older generations, largely due to changing cultural norms around vulnerability. Digital technology can be both a blessing and a curse. One of the benefits of social media is the space it creates where sharing personal struggles is not only accepted but sometimes even encouraged. Unlike previous generations, who were often taught to hide

3. WEAKNESS

imperfections, younger individuals are more likely to share their struggles, both online and in real life.

One area I've seen an increasing vulnerability in teenagers and young adults is mental health. Our city has a mental health support group called the "Underdogs Club" that gathers together for prayer, discussion, and coaching. The stigma that once surrounded topics like anxiety, depression, and failure is far less prominent with the next generation. In contrast, older generations may have internalized a more reserved or "tough" approach to personal struggles, which could lead to less awareness about their weaknesses.

You don't have to hit rock bottom to learn this lesson. It's okay to need help. Being aware of your weaknesses is a strength. It sounds like a paradox, but it's true. Weakness in and of itself is not the strength; awareness is the key. If you are weak in a particular area and unaware, it's called a blind spot. If you have a flaw and pretend it's not there, it's called pride. Identifying your weaknesses and embracing limits will allow you to depend on God and other people. The power of God is perfected in your weakness.

If you are young, you are probably acutely aware of your weaknesses. Maybe you've had homework assignments returned bleeding with red ink from grammatical errors. You're used to getting report cards in school that clearly state areas of growth. Maybe you started a job where you had no idea what you were doing. Join the club. Some of the worst advice in these situations is, "Fake it till you make it." Instead of pretending to know what you're doing, I suggest an alternative: own your weakness.

GIDEON: WEAK WARRIOR

Gideon is a fantastic example of weakness. He's the best at not being the best. When we meet Gideon in Judges 6, he is hiding grain in a winepress because he is afraid that his enemies will steal his food. He doesn't want the bullies to take his lunch.

The bullies, in this case, were the Midianites. Israel and Midian had a love-hate relationship. Sometimes they loved each other and other times not so much. The Midianites poured forth from the wilderness of Sinai and were taking food from the Israelites. The Midianites were like a countless hoard of locusts that devoured any crops they found.

Israel cried out to God in repentance, and he raised up a hero to deliver them. Yet God didn't pick the biggest or the strongest. He picked Gideon. The angel of the Lord showed up on Gideon's doorstep and said, "The LORD is with you, O mighty man of

3. WEAKNESS

valor" (Judges 6:12). This description hardly fits the trembling man playing hide-and-seek. Amazingly, the angel described the man God was calling him to be, not the man he currently was. Isn't that amazing? God sees beyond your current capacity, to the person he created you to be.

Instead of being flattered or honored by the angel, Gideon used this as an opportunity to express his doubt. He wanted to know why God had allowed Midian to pillage the land. Where was God? Why had he allowed this to happen? Would God answer their cries for help?

The angel didn't answer any of Gideon's questions, but he did solve his problem. He told Gideon that God would save Israel—and he would use Gideon to do it.

Gideon responded, "Please, Lord, how can I save Israel? Behold, my clan is the weakest in Manasseh, and I am the least in my father's house" (Judges 6:15). Already Gideon has built quite the resume. Fear? Check. Doubt? Check. Insecurity? Check. Even though God saw a mighty warrior, all Gideon could see was the least in his family. His problem wasn't that he was unaware of his weaknesses. His problem was that they were all he could see. Gideon's fixation on his flaws was shrinking his faith and derailing his calling.

The angel knew that Gideon was struggling. So he offered some assurance: "But I will be with you, and you shall strike the Midianites as one man" (Judges 6:16). I love how the assurance that God gives is not dependent on our strength.

He doesn't say, "If you can dream it, you can do it!"

He doesn't say, "You're stronger than you think you are!"

He says, "I will be with you."

It's a shift in focus from our ability to God's ability. God's strength is greater than our weaknesses. It's the people who are too busy pretending they are strong that never rely on God. This is why we see God often choose the young, lowly, inexperienced, uneducated, fearful, and the list goes on. It's because these people have to depend on God. They don't have any other choice because they know they can't do it on their own. Then when they do accomplish great things, God alone gets the glory.

The apostle Paul understood the paradox of weakness as a strength. He wrote this concerning his struggle with a physical ailment: "Therefore I will boast all the more gladly of my weaknesses, so that the power of Christ may rest upon me. For the sake of Christ, then, I am content with weaknesses, insults, hardships, persecutions, and calamities. For when I am weak, then I am strong" (2 Corinthians 12:9b-10). Paul knew that God's power

3. WEAKNESS

is perfected in our weaknesses. Gideon would have to learn this lesson the hard way.

God called Gideon to two formidable tasks. First, he told Gideon to tear down the local altar to Baal and cut down the Asherah pole. These were places of worship for false gods. Worshipping Baal and Asherah was wrong because they are false gods (see the Ten Commandments). The worship associated with them was also very immoral. It's easy to see why God wanted Gideon to clear the town. If we're going to be used by God, we have to be devoted to God.

The only problem is that these shrines belonged to Joash—Gideon's dad. By destroying the pagan places of worship, Gideon would be choosing God not only over his community but over his own family. It was a risky decision that could cost him his life. To Gideon's credit, he went through with the plan. Late at night, he gathered some friends to help him with his God-ordained vandalism. Although an angry mob formed the following day, Joash stood up for his son, and Gideon lived to fight another day.

After Gideon proved his devotion to God, it was time for the real challenge. The second difficult task God appointed Gideon to was to assemble an army and drive out the Midianites. Clothed with the Spirit, Gideon traveled around the land sounding the trumpet

WHAT ARE YOU WAITING FOR?

for battle. Miraculously, he recruited 32,000 troops for war! This army was a drop in the bucket compared to the countless hoards of Midianites, but it was better than nothing. Things were starting to look up—until Gideon decided to test God.

What takes place next in the story made Gideon famous. It is his weakness. He asked God for a sign—not once, but twice. Gideon placed a piece of wool out overnight and said that if the fleece was wet with dew, but the ground around it was dry, he would know that God is faithful. Gideon woke up the following day to find damp wool and dry ground. Still unsure, he asked God to reverse the sign. Once again, God accommodated him: dry wool and wet ground. Finally, Gideon relented and agreed to follow through with fighting the Midianites.

To be clear, this is not an example for us to follow. A better example of faith would be to obey God without putting him to the test. Gideon shows us what not to do. What's even more surprising than Gideon's unbelief is that God gave him the signs. God meets us where we are at, weaknesses and all. We are all too often like the father who doubted Jesus could heal his son, saying, "I believe; help my unbelief!" (Mark 9:24). It's our faith, not God's faithfulness, that needs to be tested. After Gideon tested God, God tested Gideon. He took the one thing Gideon

3. WEAKNESS

had going for him, a sizable army, and whittled it down to almost nothing. If Gideon goes on to win, it will be clear who gets the glory.

God directed Gideon to make a first round of eliminations. The first elimination was any soldier who was afraid to go into battle. Gideon made the announcement, and 22,000 men volunteered in a flash to go back home. Gideon was feeling increasingly uneasy at this point. Yet God said, "Still too many."

The second elimination had to do with how people drank water. God instructed Gideon to go down to the Spring of Harod and pay attention to how people drank. Anyone drinking face first in the water would be sent home. Anyone cupping the water with their hands could stay. This time, 9,700 men were told to return home, leaving Gideon with only 300 soldiers against the countless Midianites. God had turned Gideon's one strength into a weakness.

The night of the battle arrived, and Gideon devised a battle plan that sounded equally as insane as Joshua leading his troops around and around the walls of Jericho. Instead of swords, he equipped his soldiers with torches, trumpets, and empty jars. The army of 300 split up into three companies of 100 and surrounded the Midianite camp. When Gideon gave the signal, the soldiers broke the jars, blew the trumpets, and shouted, "For the Lord and for Gideon!"

What a terrifying way to wake up in the middle of the night! God caused a panic to spread through the camp. The Midianites picked up their swords and began fighting one another. Three hundred Israelites chased the host of Midianites out of the land. God brings strength out of weakness.

> **GOD BRINGS STRENGTH OUT OF WEAKNESS.**

LEARNING WEAKNESS

Everybody has weaknesses, but not everyone is aware of them. The more success you've experienced, the harder it can be to see your flaws. Success has a way of fogging up the bathroom mirror. If you've made money, been promoted, or gained followers, you probably got there by focusing on your strengths. Maybe people in your life validated your giftings—and this is great. The problem is that self-reliant leaders limit their impact because they don't rely on God or others. If you want to reach your full potential, you will need to wipe down the mirror and take a good honest look at yourself, warts and all.

Find your weaknesses before they find you. Ignoring your shortcomings won't make them go

3. WEAKNESS

away. Instead, they'll end up showing up at the most inopportune moments. In times of stress or frustration, your weaknesses will show their ugly faces. You might think you are reasonably patient until you get caught in traffic on the way to work. You tell everyone that you are a "people person," but then you have a group project with classmates you can't stand.

There are two ways to learn about your weaknesses. In humility, you can find them yourself, or they will find you. The second option usually involves humiliation.

I'm a great driver. At least, I like to think I am. I have a near-perfect record. Other than my run-in with a landscaping rock, the only other accident to my name is with a parked car. The summer after I graduated high school, I worked at a carpet store. Every day I cut the carpet, loaded it in the box truck, and delivered it to the job site. After one delivery, I backed up the box truck onto a quiet neighborhood street when I suddenly heard a *crunch!* Even though I could see out of my side windows, the vehicle didn't have a rear-view mirror to alert me of the parked car. Here's the thing about blind spots: you can't see them.

Our weaknesses are like blind spots. If we knew they were there, we probably would have done something about them by now. Although you may not know your faults, chances are the people around you see them clear as day. If you want to know the truth:

1. Ask the people closest to you for feedback.
2. Don't argue or make excuses when they share.
3. Have enough humility to listen and be honest about the parked car you just crashed into.

As painful as it might be now, these steps will save you exponentially down the road.

Ask for help. It makes me happy that the first word all three of my daughters said was "dad." It was either that or "dog." I'm not exactly sure. Parents focus on teaching their kids the critical words: *food, water, please, night-night*. Among the top ten first words we taught our kids was *help*. Do you realize we have to learn to ask for help? We tend to try things on our own. It's only after frustration, despair, temper tantrums, and tears that we finally come crying to mom and dad. I'm not just talking about kids. Many adults could use a refresher course in asking for help.

For many people, help is a four-letter word. It's easy to spell but hard to say. We're worried that by asking for help, we are exposing our weaknesses. And don't worry, that's exactly what we are doing. But we'll never get help from anyone if we aren't willing to ask for it.

3. WEAKNESS

The surprising gift of asking for help is that in return for the vulnerability we display, we receive more than help; we get a friend. Nothing binds people together in unity more than bearing each other's burdens. Think about veterans who talk about going into battle together. It's not just the trauma of war that creates brothers in arms. It is the tangible expression of standing next to someone who has your back.

Start practicing in prayer. Jesus taught that God is a good Father who wants to give us good gifts. Even though God already knows what we need, he asks us to ask him. First thing in the morning, talk through the events of your day with God. Ask him to help you with the stuff that intimidates you. You'll be surprised how a simple practice like this can change everything.

We also need to ask people for help. What are we so afraid of? Worst case scenario, the person says "no." Maybe they judge you for not being able to figure it out on your own. So what? Best case scenario, they say "yes." One of the simpler ways to practice asking for help is to ask for input. I often take out my headphones at work and talk through sermon ideas with co-workers. I usually end my pitch by saying something like, "What do you think?" or "Does that make sense?" Have a friend proofread an email or ask someone older for relationship advice. Doing these things will help you create a culture of collaboration everywhere you go.

Confess and apologize. "Sorry" is an agonizing word for many people to say. Once we identify our weaknesses, we'll become aware of how we've wronged people and God. The temptation with shortcomings is to sweep them under the rug. Hiding is the oldest trick in the book. Adam and Eve started playing hide and seek with God the moment they sinned. No one ever grew by hiding their failures in the bushes.

Pastor Carey Nieuwhof wisely comments, "Here's what I've realized in my life: confession and progress are inexorably linked. You won't address what you don't confess."[12]

Confessing is saying, "I was wrong." Apologizing is saying, "I'm sorry." If you want to face your weaknesses, you have to start owning what you do wrong. Remember what God had Gideon do before he took on the Midianites? He made him tear down the altars to false gods. It's impossible to follow God and follow the world at the same time. God needed Gideon to repent. There are probably things you need to turn from as well.

Whenever I got in trouble as a kid, my parents always made me say, "I'm sorry." I distinctly remember my dad teaching me that "sorry means you won't do it again." Don't get me wrong; I would often do it again.

3. WEAKNESS

But at least I resolved not to. The point of identifying our shortcomings is not to accept them and move on. It is to stop ignoring our flaws so that we can grow. Confession and apologizing will help you restore relationships and learn how to do it better the next time.

LEVERAGING WEAKNESS

Focus on your strengths. Weaknesses show us what things we are wasting our time on. Most academic settings teach kids to be well-rounded. If you aren't good at math, then that's where you'll usually spend most of your study time. I think this is a mistake. Don't get me wrong; there is some value in being generally good at basic skills. Yet we can quickly become a jack of all trades, master of none.

By default, we drift into what Richard Koch calls the 80/20 principle: "The 80/20 Principle asserts that a minority of causes, inputs, or effort usually lead to a majority of the results, outputs, or rewards. Taken literally, this means that, for example, 80 percent of what you achieve in your job comes from 20 percent of the time spent. Thus for all practical purposes, four-fifths of the effort—a dominant part of it—is largely irrelevant."[13] We can leverage our weaknesses by being aware of them—and by spending less time on them. If you try to be good at everything, you won't be great at anything. Try focusing on your areas of most significant impact. You'll probably never become focused enough to spend 100% of your time on your strengths. The math homework still needs to get done. But imagine what would happen if you flipped the ratio and spent 80% of your time cultivating things you are really good at? You'd be able to sharpen your skills and activate your giftings.

Get creative. Constraints lead to creativity. When you are operating from a place of insufficiency, you have to work with what you've got. God intentionally put Gideon in a position of weakness. He was not going to win with muscle power, so he had to get creative. Instead of swords, Gideon equipped his army with pots and trumpets. It was a crazy idea—so crazy that it worked. There's no way Gideon would have tried anything like this if he still had the original 32,000 soldiers.

> **CONSTRAINTS LEAD TO CREATIVITY.**

You can get creative, too. Stop making excuses and start taking steps. Identify the constraints facing you or your team and think through ways around the wall. Here's a hint: what you've always done likely won't work. The classic definition of insanity is doing the same thing and expecting different results. You are going to have to embrace your limitations and find fresh ways forward.

3. WEAKNESS

A few years ago, I had to get creative when my wife and I talked about having kids. We had bought a house. Then we got a dog. The next logical step was a baby. My biggest roadblock was that I wanted to go to seminary and get a master's degree. Many of my college friends had gone to graduate school, and I always pictured it as my next step. I imagined moving to another state, taking time off work, and restarting our life somewhere. My plan didn't resonate with Shaina.

For weeks we had an ongoing fight in our marriage. It wasn't an explosive fight with screaming matches. It was more like a slow burn. She wanted a baby, and I wanted to go to school. Both required a chunk of money (which we didn't have), and both put significant demands on our time. Every time the topic of kids or school came up, we each left the conversation frustrated. It seemed like these conflicting goals were mutually exclusive.

Then, one day, an ad popped up on my computer for an online program at Grand Canyon University in Phoenix, Arizona. Ever notice how the internet always knows exactly what advertisements to show you? I didn't know a single person who had done seminary exclusively online (this was before it was cool). Reluctantly, I sent over an inquiry email, but after a phone call with an enrollment counselor, I was sold.

WHAT ARE YOU WAITING FOR?

Less than two years later, I graduated with my Master of Arts in Christian Ministry. I worked full-time at the church during the day and did my schoolwork late into the night. We stayed in Boise, and our daughter Lily was born one month before I finished the program. I've still never been to Phoenix! The outcome was different than either Shaina or I imagined, but now we can't picture it going any other way. Your creative solution is just around the corner. It might take days or weeks of wrestling, but you'll find it if you keep looking.

Rely on others. Weakness is admitting that we don't have it together and that we need help. As humans, we are communal beings that only truly flourish when we help each other. And we'll never get help from anyone if we aren't willing to ask for it. The beautiful thing about community is that everyone is different.

When you are young and inexperienced, you can't afford to be self-reliant. You don't know what you are doing, and you know it. In moments like these, find someone older and more experienced than yourself. Ask them if they'd be willing to meet with you and teach you what they've learned along the way. These people are called *mentors*. They are the ones who can offer you wisdom to show you where you are going.

You are also going to need traveling companions. These are your peers who are there for you. The sad

3. WEAKNESS

reality is that many leaders don't have close friends. Everyone may know their name, but no one really knows what is going on in their life. Don't make this same mistake. Spend time cultivating relationships with the people you are on the journey with. Classmates, co-workers, and neighbors can become some of your best advocates.

When you find yourself in a pinch, don't hesitate to reach out to these people. Believe it or not, they want to help you. You are giving other people the opportunity to use their gifts for a greater purpose. You value people by showing them that they are needed. When the time comes, you will be there for them as well.

Throughout changes in family and school, life continued with the White Witch. She would break down, and I would replace the alternator. Round and round we went. My wife and I were still paying off student loans and didn't have the money for a newer vehicle. Then one Wednesday night, the unthinkable happened.

It was youth group, and I was a youth pastor at the time. The evening began as usual—leader meeting, hang out with students, then worship time. I was looking forward to youth group this night in particular because I didn't have any major responsibilities. Someone else was teaching, so I had the opportunity to relax. Then out of

WHAT ARE YOU WAITING FOR?

the blue, they called Shaina and me up on stage in front of two hundred junior high and high school students.

My brother (and co-worker), Andrew, was on the microphone sharing about how much Shaina and I did for the youth ministry. Shaina was one of our best leaders. She went above and beyond in mentoring her students. When her small group members were seniors in high school, she even took her girls on a mission trip to Mexico. Andrew talked about how I poured my heart and soul into teaching students. I worked tirelessly to prepare sermons and plan events that engaged students in unique ways. I was starting to get embarrassed by all the public compliments. Then just when I thought things couldn't get more uncomfortable, they blindfolded us.

Two students spun us around like we were about to attack a piñata at a child's birthday party. Then they led us outside of the building. We had no idea what was going on. Andrew told us they had a surprise for us. On the count of three, we were supposed to take off our blindfolds. *One. Two. Three!*

Sitting in front of our eyes was a 2008 Subaru Outback. It was a *massive* upgrade at the time. This vehicle was a decade newer than the White Witch and had less than half of the mileage. A bunch of people from the church had heard about our ongoing car troubles. They donated money to buy the Outback for

3. WEAKNESS

us outright. They even pitched in the extra cash to pay for registration fees. To this day, I am still completely blown away by this gift.

Despite all the nice things Andrew said on stage, we didn't deserve this gift. We didn't earn it. A loving community showed us grace. This gift turned out to be genuinely life-changing. Once we paid off student loans, we saved for a down payment on our house instead of saving for a new car. Years later, the Outback is still going strong. We've driven it on vacations, through snowstorms, and to the hospital for when each of our kids was born.

This extravagant gift was born out of weakness. Although it wasn't something I asked for, I had to humble myself enough to accept the gift. Whatever your weaknesses are, embrace them. You can stop pretending that everything is fine. When you let God and people into the hopeless parts of your life, you'll discover a great paradox. You are at your strongest when you know your weakness.

THINK ABOUT IT

Growth takes time. Before you move on, slow down long enough to reflect, journal, or discuss these questions:

WHAT ARE YOU WAITING FOR?

1. Do you have an easy or difficult time asking others for help? Why do you think that is?
2. What would the people who know you best say that your top 3 weaknesses are? (If you're not sure, ask them.)
3. Are there any mistakes or wrongdoings that you need to apologize for? When and how are you going to deal with these situations?
4. Who are the regular people in your life from whom you can ask for help? Is there anyone else that you should be asking to help you, but you haven't yet?
5. What are the constraints you face when trying to accomplish your ambitions? Instead of complaining, how can you get creative and find new solutions?
6. What strengths do you need to double down on? How can developing your top strengths actually help you go farther?

4
CALLING

"We were meant to live for so much more. Have we lost ourselves?" —Switchfoot

I have a friend named Andrew Green. When he was 25 years old, he found himself wrestling with his faith. In his own words, "I was doing all this Christian stuff, but I became aware that I wasn't following Jesus."

It didn't matter that he worked as a youth pastor at a church plant or taught part-time at a private Christian school. He felt the searing hot words of Isaiah 58 condemning God's people for participating in religious activity but neglecting to care for the oppressed. Andrew craved the pure religion of James 1:27 to care for the orphans and widows.

WHAT ARE YOU WAITING FOR?

During this time of holy discontent, Andrew read two books that wrecked his world. The first was *Love Does: Discover a Secretly Incredible Life in an Ordinary World* by Bob Goff. The second was *Kisses from Katie: A Story of Relentless Love and Redemption* by Katie Davis Majors. Both of these books champion the powerful idea of loving people like Jesus did. They both also happen to center around Uganda.

Andrew had to do something. He decided a trip to Uganda was a good starting place. Why not dive in headfirst? Andrew found a group of six other people and started planning a short-term mission trip. His goal was to experience faith outside of the American bubble.

The trip cost $1,800 that Andrew didn't have. So he started fundraising—but soon realized that he wasn't very good at it. The day of the deadline approached, and his bank account was still $1,000 short. If he didn't raise the money, he couldn't go on the trip. Andrew remembers sitting at home repeatedly hitting the refresh button on his gofundme.com page. Nothing happened.

In a last-ditch effort to make some extra cash, Andrew decided to go to downtown Boise and play guitar in the streets. He probably wouldn't get everything he needed, but it was more productive than wallowing in self-pity.

4. CALLING

No sooner did Andrew unpack his guitar than a businessman walked up and asked him what he was doing. Andrew explained his dream and the fundraising predicament that stood in his way. The mysterious stranger told Andrew to follow him. The next thing he knew, Andrew was walking into an impressive office building in downtown Boise. He felt like he was at Google headquarters.

"Wait here," the stranger commanded as he went into his office. When he came out, he handed Andrew a check for $1,000. Andrew was starting to believe that nothing is impossible for God. Little did he know that God was just getting started.

Andrew and the rest of the Uganda team spent the first half of the trip in an orphanage taking care of kids. He describes these days as "holding babies and wiping butts." There are certainly more prestigious activities, but somebody has to do it. It was here that Andrew first experienced the depths of human brokenness. Parents had abandoned these kids, and many of the kids had HIV.

During the second half of the trip, Andrew met a couple named Robert and Millie. They had recently moved to a new city in Uganda because God told them to take care of children. Andrew sensed a kindred spirit in these two. They had no money, no plan, but still offered themselves to God.

When Andrew got back to America, he was initially frustrated with the American church for neglecting to care for the poor. He didn't know what to do about it, but he knew he had to do something. Andrew started sewing backpacks. He had no idea how to sew, but Pinterest offered excellent guidance. A local coffeeshop let him set up a small table in the corner to sell the backpacks. Each month he would send whatever he earned to Robert and Millie. The first month, it was $100.

Over time, the need grew. Andrew started a nonprofit called RUJA, which means "to dream." Robert and Millie built a house to care for more children. Next, they created a medical clinic to serve the village of Kakinga. They aren't done yet. RUJA has plans to plant a church and start a school.

Andrew, who initially had trouble scraping together enough money for a plane ticket, now oversees a nonprofit that raises $100K annually. Robert and Millie aren't just taking care of the physical needs of children but allowing these kids to dream about their future. Betty wants to be a lawyer. Harriet graduated high school and is studying to be a teacher. Jane recently completed nursing school and now works part-time as a midwife at the medical clinic.

4. CALLING

You have dreams, too. God created you on purpose for a purpose. Living out your calling is choosing to believe that you were made for more. There is work to be done in the world, and you are the one to do it.

> **GOD CREATED YOU ON PURPOSE FOR A PURPOSE.**

When we are young, we are obsessed with finding our calling. Every time I chose classes in high school, it felt like I was altering my future. Things got even trickier when it came to picking a college and narrowing down a major. It seems like the number one question people ask teenagers and young adults is, "What's next?" When you're young, you can't help but think about the future.

Calling may not seem like a skill, but it is. Your sense of calling is only as strong as your ability to listen. As we get older, we don't become less called to God's work in the world. Often, though, we do stop listening as carefully. Every day we are surrounded by signposts pointing us toward purpose and meaning. Sadly, many people ignore the direction of the Holy Spirit, chalking God-ordained circumstances up to chance. Seeing nothing more than coincidence becomes the enemy of calling. After years of working the daily grind, it's easy to lose our sense of wonder and view the world in dull shades of beige. A definite way to lose your calling is to stop looking for it.

Even if you have forgotten your calling (or you've never known it), you can find it! Every single day there are good works that God created you to do. There is no one quite like you. You are a unique combination of ingredients that come together to impact the world. As long as you are willing, God will use you.

ESTHER: BEAUTY QUEEN

Esther is one of two books in the Bible that never explicitly mentions God. Yet God's fingerprints are all over Esther's story. You might be able to resonate if you've ever had trouble seeing God's hand at work in your life. But even if you've never encountered a *burning bush,* you are still walking on holy ground.

The story takes place in Susa, the capital of Persia, during the reign of King Xerxes. A Jewish man named Mordecai was living in Susa. He was old enough to remember when the Babylonian King Nebuchadnezzar destroyed Jerusalem and carried many inhabitants to the empire's far reaches. When the Persians came to power, they took a different approach toward conquered people groups. Starting with the decree of Cyrus, Jews were allowed to return to Jerusalem. The complete return

4. CALLING

would take decades, and even then, many Jews would choose their new life outside the Promised Land.

King Xerxes liked to party. The first chapter of Esther begins with a seven-day drunken bash put on by the king. Everything was over the top. Servants decorated the palace garden with fine linens, marble, gold, silver, and pearls. The king served drinks in fancy golden goblets. King Xerxes even made an official decree that there was no drinking limit. Translation: "Let's party!"

By the last day of the feast, King Xerxes had partied a little too hard. He made the mistake of ordering his wife, Queen Vashti, to dress up and show off her beauty to everyone. She wasn't having it. The king's solution was to banish Vashti from his presence forever. Then he issued a decree for all wives to obey their husbands no matter what (Xerxes liked decrees).

After Xerxes came out of his drunken stupor, he realized he no longer had a wife. What had he done? He couldn't take it back now. It was Persian law that the king's orders were irrevocable. His advisors came up with a brilliant idea. They would hold a beauty contest with all the eligible maidens in the land. Whichever girl Xerxes thought was the hottest would become the next queen of Persia. You can't make this stuff up.

Enter Esther. She was Mordecai's much younger (and much more attractive) cousin. He had been raising

WHAT ARE YOU WAITING FOR?

her since her parents died. Before Esther went to the palace for the contest, Mordecai instructed her not to reveal her Jewish heritage. She listened to her cousin and spent the next year living in the palace harem undergoing beauty treatments. Esther was so beautiful already that she hardly needed twelve minutes to prepare, let alone twelve months.

No sooner did Esther enter the palace than did she catch the eye of Hegai, one of the eunuchs in charge of the harem. He gave her special treatment, and soon she rose to the top position in the harem. When it came time for Esther to be presented before Xerxes, she followed Hegai's instructions exactly. It worked! Esther was named the new queen of Persia. Yet, unlike a Disney movie, that wasn't when the credits rolled and they lived happily ever after. Esther's story was far from over.

The villain of our story is a man named Haman. He was a descendant of the Amalekites, an enemy of Israel for hundreds of years. Haman hated the Jews. Unfortunately for Mordecai, Esther, and any other Jew living in the Persian Empire, Haman was second in command. Xerxes had even decreed (I told you he loved decrees) that people should bow down to Haman in the streets. Most people did. Mordecai is not most people.

When Haman heard that Mordecai would not bow down, he was angry. When he found out that Mordecai

4. CALLING

was a Jew, he was furious. Haman set out not only to punish Mordecai but to destroy all of the Jews. He rolled the dice to decide on which date the Jews should die. (In Hebrew, dice is called a Pur. Tuck that away for later.) Once he decided on the thirteenth day of the twelfth month, Haman went to King Xerxes with his plan. Like a puppet master, Haman convinced Xerxes to issue a (you guessed it) decree to destroy every Jew in the empire.

When Mordecai learned of the impending doom for his people, he tore his clothes, put on sackcloth and ashes, and wept. As news of the royal order spread throughout the empire, Jewish communities responded the same way. Meanwhile, Esther was safe and sound in the palace. She heard the news that the Jews were mourning but remained oblivious as to why. She even sent Mordecai a new set of clothes to try and cheer him up.

This token act of kindness sparked a correspondence between Mordecai and Esther. The messenger Hathach played the middleman. Mordecai sent a copy of the decree and pleaded with Esther to use her position as queen to persuade the king to change his mind. She responded by explaining her predicament. The punishment for entering the inner court of the king uninvited was death. Xerxes could choose to pardon her intrusion by extending the royal scepter. He also might not. Esther remembered how things ended for the last queen.

Mordecai responded with a desperate call to action:

"Do not think to yourself that in the king's palace you will escape any more than all the other Jews. For if you keep silent at this time, relief and deliverance will rise for the Jews from another place, but you and your father's house will perish. And who knows whether you have not come to the kingdom for such a time as this?" (Esther 4:13-14)

Mordecai feared for Esther's life as well. She was like a daughter to him. If her true identity became known, she would suffer the same fate as all the other Jews. Mordecai also demonstrated deep faith at this moment. He believed that even if their plan failed, nothing could stop God's plan of salvation. Then he hit her with a question about calling. Maybe God put her in this position for such a time as this.

Esther thought about the events of her life. Why was she still alive though her parents had died? Why did she come to live with her cousin in the Persian capital? Why did God create her to be so beautiful? Why did she gain favor with everyone in the palace? Why was she

4. CALLING

queen? Looking at each event individually, we might be tempted to call it merely a coincidence. But when you zoom out and see the whole picture, it is clear God was calling Esther. The future was still uncertain, but Esther became convinced this was her purpose.

"I will go to the king, though it is against the law, and if I perish, I perish," she responded (Esther 4:16). If I die, I die. Esther coined that saying. When she said those words, she meant them. She was willing to follow through on God's calling even if it cost her life.

Thankfully, it didn't. Long story short, the rest of the book of Esther records how the plan worked! At a private dinner with King Xerxes and Haman, Esther revealed that she was a Jew. This great reveal dramatically reversed the fates of Haman and Mordecai. Haman was executed. Xerxes issued a new decree which allowed the Jews to defend themselves on the thirteenth day of the twelfth month. Mordecai became the king's righthand man. The Jews were saved.

The Jews started celebrating a new holiday called "Purim" to commemorate their deliverance. The feast is named after a Pur. Remember the thing Haman cast to decide the day of destruction? God knew the dice would land on the thirteenth day of the twelfth month. Nothing can surprise God. He was working behind the

WHAT ARE YOU WAITING FOR?

scenes the whole time in subtle and imperceptible ways. It's extraordinary how God often uses ordinary events to protect and deliver his people.

> **HE WAS WORKING BEHIND THE SCENES THE WHOLE TIME.**

FIND YOUR CALLING

Knowing what you are made to do remains a mystery for the majority of people. Instead of figuring it out, most people have as their highest ambition the American dream of a spouse, a house, 1.9 kids, and a 401K. Don't be like most people. Wrestling with the following three questions will help you demystify your calling.

What Do You Care About? Everyone has different passions. Notice the things that excite you. These passions are an indication of where God is leading you to get involved. There's an old saying, "Choose a job you love, and you'll never work a day in your life." I'm not so sure this is true. I love my job, and there are plenty of days that I come home exhausted. However, when you genuinely care about what you are working on, it will get you through the hard times.

I love art, music, running, biking, teaching, nature, and Jesus. I don't know of a career where I can do all of those things simultaneously. You won't be able to pursue

4. CALLING

all of your interests equally. Over time, one or two will rise to the surface as the most important things. After I graduated high school, I was sure I would become a math teacher and running coach. I would get to do two of my passions. The first thing I did out of high school was a year at Bible college. It was there that I realized my love for Jesus was more important than my love of running. That one year of Bible school turned into four. To this day, I'm still teaching the Bible instead of algebra.

On the flip side, pay attention to the things that make you angry. If a specific kind of injustice consistently triggers you, God may be stirring your unrest for a reason. Andrew Green was enraged at apathy toward the poor and oppressed. I get ticked off when I see people being misled or living in ignorance. Truth is a big part of my life's calling. What is it for you? Don't just be angry or grow calloused. Do something about it. Be part of the solution.

What Do You Have? Everyone has different gifts. What are your strengths? Our calling often works itself out in community. Hegai, the eunuch, first noticed Esther's potential to become queen. Mordecai put two and two together about Esther's divine placement to save the Jews. We need people to see the potential in us that God sees.

WHAT ARE YOU WAITING FOR?

Think back on your life. Are there conversations, comments, or compliments that stick out? You might not recognize something as a gift if it has always come naturally to you. You may be exceptionally good at a skill but think nothing of it. When other people see you do what you do, they are amazed. It's easy to shrug off compliments out of embarrassment. Don't let the praise of people go to your head, but do reflect on it. Personal assessments are great, but the most reliable feedback will come from the people who know you well.

People aren't the only ones who can help us see how we are made. God knows us even better than we know ourselves. Every gift we have comes from God anyway. Prayers of gratitude will help you take an inventory of what you have. As you name your blessings, you'll be able to process how to use those things to help others. Remember that God always blesses us so that we can be a blessing. Blessed people bless people.

God's gifts aren't limited to our talents and abilities. You may have connections with people or financial resources or be positioned in a location to make a significant impact. I grew up in Fairbanks, Alaska, hundreds of miles from the nearest ocean. God probably wasn't calling me to be a pro surfer. Take an inventory of what you have. Then use everything God has given you for his kingdom.

4. CALLING

What Have You Been Through? Everyone has a different story. Every moment of your life has shaped you to be the person you are today. Notice common threads throughout your life. Looking back at your history is the key to unlocking your destiny.

I never thought of myself as a speaker. I had no desire to be in front of crowds or become a preacher. Yet over the years, I got more and more opportunities to speak. It started in elementary school when I made it to the finals of a speech contest by memorizing Dr. Suess's *Green Eggs and Ham*. Then in junior high and high school, I consistently received good grades on class presentations without putting in much effort.

As I got older, youth leaders gave me opportunities to share campfire devotionals and lead games. By the time I was in college, I realized that what came naturally to me was anything but natural for most people. According to *Psychology Today*, approximately 25% of the population deals with glossophobia (fear of public speaking).[14] These days I speak to hundreds of people weekly.

There are things in your past that will help you discover your future. You have taken specific classes and read certain books. Unique people have poured into your life along the way. You've encountered opportunities not available to anyone else. Each of these experiences has been shaping you for something meaningful.

WHAT ARE YOU WAITING FOR?

It's not just the good things either. Every challenge you have faced has prepared you to overcome more significant challenges one day. I remember when the COVID pandemic first came to Boise, and everything was locked down. I didn't know what to do. So I went on a hike in the foothills and prayed through Psalm 91. Along the way, I remembered all the other trials I've faced in life. Then I felt the Holy Spirit telling me, "I brought you all that. I'll bring you through this." God will do the same for you. Each trial can refine you and make you stronger for what comes next.

LEVERAGE YOUR CALLING

Help Others. God's calling for you isn't just about you. Once you know what you are good at, find a way to do it for others. Esther initially rejected Mordecai's plea to go before the king. She was thinking only of her own life and the potential consequences. The thing that got her off the sidelines was realizing that she might be able to save all the other Jews.

In 2020, my wife and I started using grocery pickup. We still use this convenient service even though stores have opened back up again. The other day, I met a standout Walmart associate during pickup. Instead of simply unloading my groceries, he engaged me in conversation.

4. CALLING

He asked about the nationality of my wife's maiden name. He noticed that I bought a pineapple and recommended a tool that makes cutting pineapple easier. When he finished loading the car, he even left me with a joke of the day. Groceries aren't his primary concern. People are.

If you sell tires, you aren't just selling tires. You are helping that one person get where they are going. If you work at a bagel shop, you aren't just making bagel sandwiches. You are feeding a single mom, so she has the energy to work and take care of her kids. Look for the people. How does your work intersect with someone else's needs? I have a friend who is a manager at Black Rock Coffee Bar. Their company motto is "fuel your story." I know the motto because it's printed on all their cups. These baristas aren't just selling cups of coffee; they fuel people to write their own stories.

It should feel good when you find your purpose. But your calling is about more than self-actualization. God put you on this planet for a reason. You may not be able to help everyone in the world. Don't let that stop you from helping the one person that God puts in your path today. Love your neighbor. Like the Good Samaritan from Luke 10, don't turn a blind eye. There is nothing more rewarding than doing something for another person without a reward.

Pay the Cost. Just because we are called doesn't mean it's going to be easy. The apparent overnight success stories of celebrities give us the wrong idea. From the outside looking in, it seems like successful people walked an easy road. Justin Bieber's mom posted a video online of him singing, and then BOOM, now he's a superstar. This illusion doesn't acknowledge the countless time, energy, and money that goes into every one of these stories. There is almost certainly a cost that comes from our calling.

Back to Esther's story. Esther didn't end up paying the ultimate price of her life. But she was willing to. In an article for the *Christian Standard,* Seana Scott explains the tension that Esther must have felt. "Sometimes choosing the right thing may cost us greatly. Other times, like in the book of Esther, our integrity is vindicated and rewarded. No matter the outcome, choosing the right thing when it's the hard thing is always a good thing."[15]

If you follow your calling long enough, eventually you will find yourself at a crossroads. You will have to decide between the easy thing and the right thing. I remember the day I was approached about the possibility of Hill City Church merging with Capitol City Christian Church. That afternoon, I went on a run and asked God if he was calling me to this work.

4. CALLING

To be honest, I was extremely hesitant about the merger. I knew it would be a ton of work. I had heard horror stories of young pastors getting chewed up and spit out by congregations they stepped in to save. I wasn't sure that I was up to the challenge. I didn't hear the audible voice of God, but one thing did become clear to me by the end of the run. When he calls us, God's highest priority for us isn't comfort.

Andrew Green can attest to the cost of calling. God has always provided for RUJA along the way, but there were many moments where Andrew had an empty bank account. He recalls one humbling memory where he spent his last few dollars on a root beer. He drank his soda in sorrow before knocking on his parents' door and asking to move back in for a while.

"There were a lot of times I wanted to quit. I didn't see God's hand through the hardship and difficulty. Now it is so clear and obvious," said Andrew.

You might have moments where you want to throw in the towel. I know I have. The best things in life are rarely easy. If God calls you to it, he'll get you through it. He may not take away the pain, but he will never leave you along the way. It's going to be challenging to see God at times. When you look back, you'll see his fingerprints all over your story.

WHAT ARE YOU WAITING FOR?

Join God. While your calling won't always be easy, it shouldn't feel like trying to bust down a brick wall. If there are too many closed doors, God may be directing you away from the opportunity. Following your calling is more of an art than a science. You won't get very far trying to blaze your own trail in the world. The key is to find the places where God has already been paving a path.

Prayer is essential to notice God's hand at work. Archbishop of Manchester William Temple famously said, "When I pray, coincidences happen, and when I don't, they don't." (In other words, they aren't just coincidences.) Pray about your future. As you pray, look around. Are any opportunities opening up? Is there a need that presents itself? Did you have a unique conversation with just the right person? We need to stop seeing merely coincidences and start seeing *calling*.

Doug Paul calls these pathways "grooves of grace." In *Ready or Not,* he writes, "We need eyes to see what God is doing; where there is a supernatural ease, a pathway for kingdom breakthrough that exceeds the effort we're putting in."[16] Jesus said that apart from him, we can do nothing (John 15:5). So why do we still try to accomplish things without him? We make the biggest impact when we walk with God. Remember how the

4. CALLING

story ends: God wins. When we join him in his kingdom work, no obstacle will be able to stop us.

God is calling some of you reading this to vocational ministry. You are a future pastor, missionary, youth worker, or worship leader. Or maybe you will work in a parachurch organization that works across denominational lines. Ministry is not the most glamorous job (I can speak from experience). For whatever reason, God has entrusted us to shine his light into this dark world. There is a whole generation of church leaders who are burning out. If you don't rise to the occasion, who will?

IF YOU DON'T RISE TO THE OCCASION, WHO WILL?

God is calling others to work outside of the church. The world needs doctors, lawyers, plumbers, stay-at-home parents, and outgoing Walmart associates. There is no such thing as an unimportant job in God's kingdom. The world needs your work. Tear down the wall in your mind that separates secular from sacred callings. Your unique position will allow you to help others and share the gospel with specific people.

God is calling you. What will you say?

WHAT ARE YOU WAITING FOR?

FIND YOUR PURPOSE

You never know when you will become clear on God's calling in your life. It's going to take time, prayer, and discernment. For me, it was late at night, on a run, in the woods. I was 20 years old. The junior class at our Bible college was on a retreat in McCall, Idaho. Our assigned reading leading up to this retreat was Craig Groeschel's book *Chazown: Define Your Vision. Pursue Your Passion. Live Your Life on Purpose.* The subtitle speaks for itself.

After a long day of team-building exercises, self-assessments, and group discussions, I needed to get outside. Andrew (my brother, not Andrew Green), Jake, and I bundled up in the warmest clothes we packed and took off running into the cold winter night. As we cruised on the backroads shrouded in Ponderosa pine trees, we had nothing but headlamps to light our way.

We shared what we were processing over the weekend. One of the objectives was to create a personal vision statement for our lives. My vision statement was "to reveal truth to people about God, themselves, and the world around them so they can live more in touch with reality." I have this line committed to memory to this day.

4. CALLING

For the first time, I was able to put words to something that I had always loved. I call it the "light-bulb moment." It's the moment when someone goes from not understanding something to when it finally clicks. I tutored my friends in math throughout high school because I loved helping them get it. At the retreat, my passion for truth crystalized around God's Word.

As a pastor's kid myself, I never wanted to become a pastor. Yet here I was in my third year at Bible college. God had opened doors to get me to Boise and closed doors elsewhere. That night I shared with Andrew and Jake that I wanted to plant a church. I gave in. I went from resisting this calling to committing to it. Things seem much more real when you say them out loud.

"What about you guys?" I asked.

My confession opened the door for Andrew and Jake to share honestly. Jake talked about leading worship and being part of a church that reaches young adults. He dreamed of a church to invite his friends to without being embarrassed that they would have a bad experience. Andrew was already serving in youth ministry and expressed a desire to hang out with students for years to come. He didn't see youth ministry as a stepping stone to bigger and better things. In many ways, he was already in his sweet spot.

WHAT ARE YOU WAITING FOR?

Then the three of us began to dream together. What if our callings converged? Our gifts and passions were certainly complementary. I could preach, Andrew could disciple students, and Jake could lead worship. We could feel the excitement rising within us. It didn't matter that it was midnight; we were wide awake.

Ten years later, the three of us live this dream every day. God gave me the opportunity to plant Hill City Church in fall 2018. Although Jake worked at another church at the beginning of the year, he joined me as associate pastor a few months before the launch. Now Jake leads worship every week. Andrew also worked at another church, but he joined our team as family pastor during our first year.

It didn't always feel like I was living out my calling over the last decade. That late-night conversation in McCall would fade from my memory, but God hadn't forgotten. There were times I doubted if I would ever plant a church, much less work with two of my best friends. Now I can say without a doubt that God was with me every step of the way.

Hang in there. Even when you don't see it, God is working.

4. CALLING

THINK ABOUT IT

Growth takes time. Before you move on, slow down long enough to reflect, journal, or discuss these questions:

1. Do you have a clear or fuzzy sense about what God created you to do in the world? What would help bring God's calling more into focus?
2. What do you care about? What issues of injustice make you the angriest? What could you do about it?
3. When you work on a team, what strengths do you bring to the table? What else has God entrusted to you (possessions, relationships, knowledge, etc.)?
4. What are the top defining moments of your life (think through both the good and bad)? Where do you see God's fingerprints in the timeline of your life? How has God prepared you in the past for your future?
5. How can you help others in your current life context? Where might God take you if you were faithful in the small things every day?
6. What costs might come with your calling? Are you willing to pay them? Why or why not?

7. Where do you see God already at work in your life? What would it look like for you to join God in his mission to build the kingdom of heaven?

5
ATTENTION

"Staying calm and performing at your best when you know that any mistake could mean death requires a certain kind of mindset." —Alex Honnold[17]

We drove west into the setting sun. I was still in youth ministry at the time, and we were preparing for one of the most important events of the year. I was tired, and driving a half hour into the middle of nowhere to pick up hundreds of straw bales was not on my list of things I'd like to do.

The event was a paintball obstacle course called "The Gauntlet." Each October, we set up a maze of straw bales, plywood, cars, and whatever else we could find. Students would then mask up and try to make it from one end to the other without getting hit while snipers

WHAT ARE YOU WAITING FOR?

shot paintballs at them from a tower nearby. I still have no idea why so many students loved this event. I also have no idea why we didn't get more complaints from parents. These were the good old days of youth ministry.

That's why we were in Caldwell, Idaho. We had purchased two hundred straw bales from a farmer. Usually, people used straw for animal bedding, gardening, or harvest decorations. We had something else in mind. It was our third year doing the event, so we had to keep going bigger and better. My brother Andrew was the mastermind behind the operation. We both worked as youth pastors at the same church, but even if we didn't, I'm sure he would have found a way to rope me into helping somehow.

Truth be told, I hated The Gauntlet. I didn't like getting shot with paintballs. (Honestly, who does?) I didn't like the incredible amount of work it was to set up the obstacle course. The thing I disliked more than anything was the straw. I get pretty bad seasonal allergies. When you are transporting load after load of straw, it gets everywhere. It sticks to your clothes. It gets down in your socks and stabs your ankles for weeks to come. Whenever you lift a straw bale, part of it disintegrates and creates a cloud of dust. Yet it had to be done. There's a reason I'm not in youth ministry anymore.

5. ATTENTION

There were four of us there that night: Andrew, Dale, Harrison, and me. (My brother, Andrew, you know.) Dale was a middle-aged youth leader who grew up in rural Idaho. He was a plumber, and it seemed like he knew everyone in the valley. He knew someone who let us borrow a large flatbed trailer. Harrison was an unsuspecting youth student. He had no idea what he was getting himself into when he volunteered to help us that night. Between the two trucks and the four of us, we had incredible straw-stacking potential. Instead of making multiple trips, thirty minutes each way, we were hoping to get all the straw in one fell swoop.

Once we arrived at the farm, we got to work. We split up into two teams. Dale and Andrew took care of loading up the trailer while Harrison and I went to work loading the truck beds. As per usual, a friendly rivalry formed. Which team would pack the most straw? Andrew and Dale were cruising. They kept shouting comments like, "What's taking you guys so long?" and "We'll try and leave you some."

Harrison and I, on the other hand, were more methodical with loading our truck. He had never done it before, so he was looking to me for direction. I wanted to make sure we stacked every straw bale on top of two more in a brick pattern. If I noticed one was a little off,

WHAT ARE YOU WAITING FOR?

I would hop onto the truck and adjust it slightly. I can be a bit particular about things like this.

At one point, Harrison looked at me and said, "They're beating us."

I shrugged. "As long as the straw all gets back to the church, I'll be happy. I'd rather spend more time now getting it stacked properly and less time fixing it later."

We kept grinding away late into the night until we loaded up all two hundred straw bales. Andrew and Dale's trailer was impressive. Straw bales towered higher than I thought was possible. We definitely didn't want to drive back out for a second trip. Harrison and I didn't stack my truck nearly as high, but at least it was neatly organized. I was just happy to be finally getting out of there.

We headed back to civilization. As I pulled out behind the trailer, I felt that some of the bales might not make it back to Boise. Every bump we went over seemed to shake the structural integrity of the straw mountain to its foundation. I tried not to overthink it. Dale grew up around farms. He knew what he was doing. So away we went.

Dale sped away into the night. I drove at a casual pace with Harrison in the passenger seat. Once again, he noticed the competitive opportunity.

"Aren't you going to try to catch up?" he asked.

5. ATTENTION

"Meh. I know the way home. Besides, I'm hauling like 80 straw bales. I'd rather take my time now than have to stop if any fall off," I answered.

Then almost right on cue, we saw bale after bale lining the side of the road. Andrew and Dale's straw tower was hemorrhaging. Then we saw blue and red flashes of a police car parked next to their trailer up ahead. I couldn't believe my eyes. The straw that we had seen along the road wasn't even the worst of it. Half of the straw tower had fallen over and was now sitting in the middle of this country road. Thankfully, Dale knew the policeman. He let us off with a warning, and they didn't even make us come back and clean it up. We salvaged what we could and made it back to the church with the remaining straw.

That night taught me the valuable leadership skill of attention. Attention is simply thinking about what you are doing. It has to do with being present in the moment and not taking shortcuts. Attention may not be the fastest way to get the job done. But it reliably gets the job done right the first time. More time now, less time later.

Young leaders more naturally have to pay attention because they don't know what they are doing. While many would view this as a weakness, attention is an incredible strength. You cannot rush some activities.

WHAT ARE YOU WAITING FOR?

Researcher Liz Wiseman believes attention is a helpful resource that rookies possess. She writes, "Because rookies are disoriented and lack know-how, they are forced into a sense-making mode that causes them to pay close attention to their environment and reach out to others for guidance."[18] We focus way more on something when we haven't done it before. We've also all done things haphazardly. It's easy to speed through familiar tasks and make too many mistakes. Our muscle memory takes over, and we take shortcuts to get things done quickly. What if *quick* isn't the most important metric of success? When *quality* is the goal, it pays to pay attention.

> **YOUNG LEADERS MORE NATURALLY HAVE TO PAY ATTENTION.**

SAMUEL: ATTENTIVE APPRENTICE

Before Israel was a kingdom, there was Samuel. He was a miracle baby. His mother, Hannah, persistently prayed for God to open her womb and give her a child. She was desperate. In an honor-shame culture, her ability to provide heirs to continue the family shaped her identity. It got to the point where she promised God that she would dedicate her child to serving him if he granted her request.

5. ATTENTION

Sure enough, Samuel was born, and Hannah made good on her commitment. As soon as Hannah weaned him, she dropped him off at the temple to be raised by Eli, the high priest. You can imagine the surprise on Eli's face. He was an older man with adult children of his own. Now he was responsible for another one. Each year Hannah would visit the temple with a new priestly outfit for little Samuel, but Eli would raise him the rest of the year.

One day when Samuel was still a little boy, he heard something. It was the middle of the night, and he heard a voice say, "Samuel!" Thinking it was Eli calling to him, Samuel got up at once and ran to Eli's bedside. To his surprise, Samuel found Eli fast asleep. A very groggy Eli sent Samuel straight back to bed.

Samuel was almost drifting off to sleep when he heard something a second time. Again, "Samuel!" Once again, he went running to Eli, who again sent the boy back to bed.

No sooner did Samuel get back to his bed than he heard the voice a third time. He ran back to Eli. At this point, Eli discerned that Samuel was hearing the voice of God. Eli instructed Samuel to respond the next time, saying, "Speak, LORD, for your servant hears" (1 Samuel 3:9). Samuel was astounded. The visions and prophetic words were infrequent during those days.

Why would God be speaking to him? After all, he was just a kid.

Samuel went back to bed for the fourth time. This time he was paying attention. When he heard the voice calling out to him, he responded, "Speak, LORD, for your servant hears" (1 Samuel 3:10). Now that God had Samuel's attention, he gave him his first prophecy. And it wasn't a happy prophecy. God told Samuel of his plan to punish Eli's household for the sins of his corrupt sons. Samuel listened closely. The following day he didn't mix words when he relayed the message to Eli. It wouldn't be the last word Samuel would hear from God. Samuel went on to have a long career in Israel as a prophet, priest, and judge. He would be a key player in ushering the kingdom of Israel into reality. He saw kings rise and fall. It all started by paying attention to what God wanted to do through him.

MOVING TOO FAST

If you want to pay attention, you have to slow down. Hurry kills attention. Mistakes abound when we have a tight deadline. We stop being present for the people in our lives when we are moving too fast. Perhaps the deadliest consequence of a fast-paced life is that we lose touch with our hearts. John Mark Comer says it like

5. ATTENTION

this: "Both sin and busyness have the exact same effect—they cut off your connection to God, to other people, and even to your own soul."[19]

Many people would love to hear from God but feel like he's distant. I would argue that God is speaking all the time, but he often speaks in a still small voice. Maybe we don't have the attention to hear. Samuel heard God's voice three times before he knew it was him. It wasn't until he was intently listening that he was able to get the message. Are you paying attention? Or are you moving at light speed through life?

Early in the morning of June 3, 2017, Alex Honnold started climbing "El Capitan." Three hours and 56 minutes later, he arrived at the top of the 7,573-foot mountain. It would be an impressive feat by itself, but that day Alex made history. Why? He did it without a rope. You can watch it on the National Geographic documentary *Free Solo*.

Even though the actual climb took around four hours, Honnold had been preparing for years. He had climbed El Cap at least fifty times over a decade. Then for two years, Alex intentionally mapped out his route. He describes the process in a TED talk:

> "As I practiced the moves, my visualization turned to the emotional component of a potential solo.

WHAT ARE YOU WAITING FOR?

Basically, what if I got up there and it was too scary? What if I was too tired? What if I couldn't quite make the kick? I had to consider every possibility while I was safely on the ground so that when the time came, and I was actually making the moves without a rope, there was no room for doubt to creep in."[20]

Alex Honnold understands the importance of paying attention. It would be better to go slow and get it right than go too fast and make a mistake. In the case of a free solo, going too fast could be a life-or-death mistake. Attention doesn't necessarily equate to caution. Free soloing a mountain is not cautious by any stretch of the imagination. It's one of the riskiest activities out there. The point isn't to stop taking risks. The point is to be present in the moment so that you minimize failure.

Many leaders believe that moving faster equals faster results. Hustle to get ahead. The last one there is a rotten egg. This mindset is a lie. It's going in the right direction that equals better results. It doesn't do you any good to be moving a hundred miles per hour in the wrong direction.

Growing up in Fairbanks, Alaska, I did a little bit of mountain bike racing. In mountain bike racing, it's all too easy to get lost in the woods. I remember one

5. ATTENTION

race vividly. I was riding my bike on this single-track trail, when eight miles into this race, I came across a guy walking his bike toward me. He had a flat tire. He stopped and told me we were two miles off course. We had both missed the turn. If I hadn't run into him, I might still be out there in the woods.

The same thing happened in the marathon I ran in Bend, Oregon. About twenty-one miles in, my brother and I were running together when we came upon a four-way trail intersection. A guy ran straight toward us. He had gotten off track by a few miles. He accidentally ran an ultra-marathon that day and was not happy about it.

More time now, less time later.

LEARNING ATTENTION

One problem many seasoned leaders face is that they hit cruise control. They rely on muscle memory to accomplish the same tasks they've been doing for years. On the one hand, this enables them to check off boxes while putting in minimal effort. On the other hand, relying too much on routine leads to mistakes and mediocrity. We can easily trade significant world-changing work for simply getting through the day.

It is much like zoning out while driving a car. Have you ever forgotten you were driving? We've all had those groggy mornings where we got in the car and didn't quite wake up until we were halfway to our destination. We relied on our familiarity with the route to take us where we were going. While you can get by going like this for a little while, you'll inevitably make mistakes. Maybe someone honked at you for sitting too long at a green light or drifting into the other lane. At that moment, what did you do? You woke up. You started paying attention. Maybe this chapter is an opportunity to wake up. HONK!

Slow down. If hurry kills attention, then the solution is simple—slow down. Think about the pace that you are living life. How much margin do you have in your day? Are you always running five minutes behind? Do you have time to breathe in between appointments? How fast do you drive? (I once had a boss who told me I didn't walk quickly enough when I took a bathroom break!) If you asked ten people how they are doing this week, my bet is most of them would say, "I'm busy." So how do we slow down?

THINK ABOUT THE PACE THAT YOU ARE LIVING LIFE.

Slowing down your pace of life ultimately comes down to priorities. You probably can't do everything you are doing and still slow down. Once you swallow this hard truth, you'll find an incredible amount of freedom. Demands pull our attention in so many different

5. ATTENTION

directions, but not all of those directions are equally important.

List your priorities. Creating a list of priorities allows us to focus on the things that matter most. These are the rocks. Once you know what the non-negotiable items are, lock them into your calendar. Always make time for your family, health (physical, spiritual, emotional, etc.), and the vocational things that only you can do.

Then figure out how much more time you have for the secondary items. These things are the sand that fills in the cracks. These items might be entertainment, hobbies, and work tasks that aren't mission-critical. Don't put too many of these things back in. If we are actually going to slow down, we need more space in our schedules.

Once you have a weekly calendar with a better rhythm, then you'll need to stick to it. To do this, you'll need to know when to say "no" to new things that try to weasel their way into your day. Try not to multi-task. Remember, the value of slowing down is to be present and focus on what you are doing. Implement boundaries with work. There may be seasons to go in early and stay late, but it shouldn't be all the time. You'll be surprised how much more you can get done when you have time to think about what you are doing.

WHAT ARE YOU WAITING FOR?

Measure twice, cut once. The building Capitol City Christian Church gave Hill City Church is worth $3 million. It's in a premium location in downtown Boise. You don't have to be a real estate expert to know what a great deal this is. While I am incredibly thankful to inherit a fully paid-off facility, there was still a cost as part of the deal. After all, the building is 110 years old. There were more than a few maintenance items that needed attention. No sooner did we move in than we began a $2 million building renovation. It's a bit of a fixer-upper.

Throughout the renovation, I learned more about construction than I ever thought I would. One of the lessons that kept coming up is the old saying, "Measure twice, cut once." There were numerous points along the way where I would walk into a room and notice something was off. On a Wednesday, I walked into the newly tiled bathrooms and realized the grout color was wrong. It was white but was supposed to be black. Not a huge deal, but I don't want to be perpetually cleaning white grout for the rest of my life. This kind of repair was a pain to fix after the fact. If we had caught this mistake before laying the grout, it would be a simple trip to the hardware store.

At one point, I overheard a contractor mention he was about to order thousands of square feet of carpet

5. ATTENTION

for the lobby and second-story classrooms. The only problem was that it was the wrong carpet. Luckily, I caught that in time. We checked the design papers and adjusted the order. Measure twice, cut once. So how did I notice a detail that a professional contractor missed? It wasn't because I had more construction experience. I was paying attention. If you want to succeed at work and life, then you need to pay attention, too.

LEVERAGE ATTENTION

Pay attention to people. Once you know how to slow down and be present in the moment, you've got to use attention to your advantage. It's not just your work that needs your attention; people need it, too. Pay attention to your family and friends. Pay attention to your co-workers and neighbors. The most important thing you have to offer the people in your life is *you*. Yet, we are so often absent either in body or in spirit. We miss another meal together or a date night or a sports game. Or even if we do show up, often we're not truly there. Distraction or busyness dominates our minds.

If you can relate to this, follow the same protocol used to cross a busy street: stop, look, and listen. What is preventing you from being there for the people in your life? Stop it. It might be overwork or an excessive hobby.

WHAT ARE YOU WAITING FOR?

For many of us, our distractions come from our phones. The world was a more straightforward place when spiral cords chained phones to the wall. We must put rules on our devices so they don't rule us. Decide when you aren't going to be on your phone—at dinner, in bed, during family game night, etc. Most smartphones even have screen time limits you can set for yourself. Make your phone work for you, not the other way around. Whatever it is, put limits on the things that are preventing you from being with the people that matter the most.

After you stop, look. Look people in the eyes. This is when we begin to unlock the power of presence. We know that eye contact is good for the soul. It isn't about having staring contests with people but having real conversations. Just compare how much time you spend a day looking at screens versus looking at people.

When you begin to slow down to see the people around you, you might notice things you missed before. You'll see your friend got a new haircut. You'll see that your co-worker is stressed. You'll see a loved one is lonely. We don't just get the grout color wrong when we rush through life. We might be missing out on the people we love the most. Looking will allow you to recalculate and change directions if needed.

5. ATTENTION

The third step is to listen. Deeply listen to people. It might be weird for them at first because it is increasingly rare in our world. Keep listening. Ask twenty questions. Then ask one more. Sometimes we feel like we need to have something interesting to say to keep the conversation going, but that's not the most important thing. It is better to be interested than interesting.

This practice is called "incarnational listening." It means "to listen at a heart level with empathy, attuned to the words and nonverbal communication of another person (i.e., so that the other person feels felt by you)."[21] Do the people in your life feel seen and felt by you?

This year, I received a tough pastoral call. An older couple had just lost their adult son. He lived a rough life and got mixed up with the wrong kind of crowd. At first, it appeared to be a drug overdose, but upon further investigation the cause of death was inconclusive. Police came in to see if it was a possible murder. Not only did this family have to grieve through the loss of a loved one, but they had to endure answering endless questions from police officers. To make matters worse, all of this happened in the middle of the COVID shutdown, so the family had to deal with the added layer of planning a funeral under tight restrictions.

WHAT ARE YOU WAITING FOR?

I called the father and asked if he would like me to come to their house for a visit. He said they would appreciate it. On the drive to their home, I realized that I had absolutely no idea what to say or do. Sure, I was the pastor, but they don't exactly train you for situations like this in Bible college. Upon arriving at the house, I sat down with the family in a dimly-lit living room. Then there was silence. I asked a question here and there, but mainly I just sat and listened. I paid attention to people who were grieving the most resounding loss of their lives. Then I closed our time together with a simple prayer and was on my way.

It would be easy to look back on that visitation and think that I should have done more. Maybe I could have shared some Bible verses and spiritual encouragement. But in reality, simple presence is just what that family needed. I know because they told me so with tears in their eyes at the funeral later that week. If you are going to give your attention to anything, give it to people.

Pay attention to God. You don't just need to take time to be present to other people; you need to be present with God. When there is too much

> **BE PRESENT WITH GOD.**

noise, we won't be able to hear ourselves think, let alone listen to the voice of God. Remember when God spoke to Samuel? It was in the stillness of the night. God spoke

5. ATTENTION

to Elijah in a still small voice (1 Kings 19:12). Many people complain that God doesn't speak to them. Maybe God is speaking, but we just aren't paying attention. As Jacob said, "Surely the LORD is in this place, and I did not know it" (Genesis 28:16). God wants to speak words of truth to you. He may want to clarify your calling and help you unlock your purpose. Your heavenly Father might remind you of your identity. The Holy Spirit might be trying to convict you and help you grow. So why don't we slow down so we can listen?

Think of the hypothetical question, "If you could have a conversation with anyone in history, who would it be?" Maybe for you, it's a president, author, or movie star. You could pick a distant relative that you never had the opportunity to meet. It could be anyone. Now imagine that person calls your phone. You can see their name on the caller ID. Would you pick it up? Of course! We wouldn't miss that conversation for the world. Yet, how many days go by in our lives without slowing down to be present with God?

Pay attention to your heart. One reason few leaders slow down is that we're afraid of what we will hear. We know there are stuffed emotions and unresolved pain bubbling beneath the surface. Maybe we know there is evil bound up in our hearts, and we'd rather medicate through distraction and busyness than get to the core of the issue. It's much easier to pretend nothing is wrong and keep living life as usual. Ignorance is bliss. Or is it?

Sooner or later, what's inside inevitably comes out. If we have hurt in our hearts, it will end up hurting the people closest to us. Unconfessed sin will come creeping back as a new temptation or the same old shame. During times of high stress or conflict, your heart spills over. Andy Stanley writes, "Eventually our heart—the real you—will outpace your attempts to monitor and modify everything you say and do. The unresolved issues stirring around undetected in your heart will eventually work their way to the surface."[22]

You don't have to let what is going on inside you burst out at the most inopportune moments. You don't have to live in ignorance. Learn to be present with yourself and God. Schedule times each day for silence and solitude. It doesn't have to be a mediation session; you can go for a walk. Buy a quality journal and spend time writing about your day. See a good counselor who can help you sort through deeper wounds. Believe me; it's worth the money. Slow down and pay attention now. I promise you won't regret it later.

5. ATTENTION

THINK ABOUT IT

Growth takes time. Before you move on, slow down long enough to reflect, journal, or discuss these questions:

1. When is a time that you made a mistake because you were going too fast? Were you able to go back and fix the mistake?
2. Do you feel like you are going in the right direction in life? How do you know? How often do you slow down and make course corrections in your life?
3. What are the immovable priorities that need to make it into your schedule every week? What are optional activities you could cut or limit so that you can experience more margin?
4. In what decisions in your life do you need to "measure twice, cut once"? What would help you think through these situations and make wise choices?
5. Who are the people in your life that need your attention? How can you stop, look, and listen to these people this week?

6. What is going on in your heart? What can you do to stay more in touch with your deeper thoughts and feelings?
7. What are the main things that distract you from listening to God? What do you need to do to eliminate those distractions so you can hear God's still small voice? Spend some time now and pray Samuel's prayer, "Speak, LORD, for your servant hears."

6
LISTENING

"She generally gave herself very good advice (though she very seldom followed it)." —Lewis Carroll

How do you know if you are ready to get married? I was asking this question at the beginning of my senior year in college. I had only been dating Shaina for six months, but I was pretty confident I wanted to spend the rest of my life with her.

I wasn't only asking myself; I sought out a few confidants for advice. The timing of an engagement isn't exactly something you post about on social media. It kind of spoils the surprise of popping the question. So I talked with my brother, a few close friends, and Danny.

Danny is a professor at Boise Bible College. He loves golf, gardening, and backpacking and he lived in Africa

WHAT ARE YOU WAITING FOR?

for a while. He is a good friend and has mentored me on and off throughout the years. We met together once a week throughout my senior year to discuss life and ministry and drink coffee.

We were at the Starbucks on Glenwood Street when I brought up marriage.

"How did you know you were ready to get married?" I asked.

"It just made sense. A dating relationship can only go in one of two directions, and I knew Traci and I were going to stay together," Danny answered. "Are you thinking of proposing to Shaina?" (A good mentor always answers your question with another question.)

"I don't know. Most of my married friends dated for a long time before getting engaged. But I'm graduating this year, and it kind of makes sense," I hesitantly fumbled through my response. It was clear I needed to think through this decision a bit more.

"There are a lot of bad reasons to get married. Some people do it because they can't stand being alone. Others get married because they want to have sex. Codependency, insecurity, the list goes on and on. Do you want to get married for a bad reason?" Danny interrogated.

6. LISTENING

Things were getting real. I ran through Danny's list of faulty marriage motivators—none resonated. I simply answered, "No."

"Do you love her?" Danny said bluntly.

"One of my favorite things to do is make Shaina smile. I would gladly sacrifice my comfort for her happiness. I can totally be myself around her. She loves God and will make a great partner in ministry. When I envision years into the future, I see Shaina in my life. So yes, I love her," I replied.

"It sounds like you have your answer," Danny smiled. It was at this exact moment that I decided to propose to Shaina. I didn't go out and do it right away. I still had to work three jobs to save enough money for an engagement ring. Then I would put together an elaborate Christmas Eve scavenger hunt. Obviously. But at that moment, I had my answer.

This interaction with Danny demonstrates the power of an honest conversation with a wise person. One of the most common answers I received when I asked friends about the proposal question was, "When you know, you know." That may be true, but it was utterly unhelpful for me. My issue at the time was that I didn't know. I needed someone to give me advice and ask me probing questions. I needed a Danny.

WHAT ARE YOU WAITING FOR?

There are moments in all of our lives where we need direction. You might be thinking through a relationship, education, or career path. When you're not sure what to do, whom do you go to for advice? Proverbs 24:6 says, "For by wise guidance you can wage your war, and in abundance of counselors there is victory."

In the digital age, social media provides no shortage of counselors. We crowdsource our decisions by throwing out a tweet and waiting for dozens of replies. Sadly, the internet hardly qualifies for "wise guidance." Quantity does not equal quality. If you want victory, you don't need more voices; you need more wise voices.

Young people have an advantage when it comes to gaining wisdom—we ask for it. We know we don't know everything, so we ask people ahead of us in life. As people grow older, they learn a thing or two. In many ways, the experience that comes with age is a good thing. However, one of the pitfalls of knowledge is it tends to make you impervious to learning new things. A know-it-all makes a lousy learner.

Listening is a superpower the best leaders have. If you can make it to the end of your life with your ears wide open, you'll have done better than most. Listening is different from hearing. You hear when sound waves pass through the ear canal and vibrate the eardrum. Listening is about processing and responding to what

6. LISTENING

you hear. Every parent has at some point raised their voice at their child, "Are you listening?!"

If it's good advice, you should listen to it. If it's terrible, tune it out. Wise people can tell the difference between the two. Fools find discernment more challenging. They might

> **LISTENING IS A SUPERPOWER THE BEST LEADERS HAVE.**

tune out something vital but listen to garbage. To be honest, it's trickier than it sounds to tell the difference. We have access to more information on our smartphones than we know what to do with.

The COVID-19 pandemic brought with it another sinister threat—an infodemic. This is "an overabundance of information—some accurate and some not—that makes it hard for people to find trustworthy sources and reliable guidance when they need it."23 Have you ever heard of #fakenews? Bloggers publish cleverly named click-bait articles without doing their research. People share a video or a post thousands of times without verifying if it's true.

Truth matters for more than philosophical reasons; it's practical. What you believe determines how you live. What you think determines how you act.

So how do you know that what you believe is actually true? All of the noise in the world becomes like wax clogging our ears. It's tempting to become cynical

WHAT ARE YOU WAITING FOR?

and stop trusting anyone altogether. This approach won't help us, either. We need guidance in life. When we begin unplugging from all the noise of the surrounding culture, we begin to realize that not all voices are equal. We don't need millions of half-baked opinions. We need a few people telling the truth.

Even if you are not a great listener, you can learn. All it takes is an ounce of humility for you and a sprinkle of wisdom on the person you're listening to.

RUTH: LOYAL WIDOW

Listening matters the most when we need to make crucial decisions. Everyone eventually comes to crossroads. It may be an earth-shattering disaster or a life-altering opportunity. Ruth lived (and listened) through both.

Ruth's story begins with a famine. There was no food in the land of Judah, so a Jewish family moved from Bethlehem (ironically named "house of bread") east to the kingdom of Moab. The mother was named Naomi, and she had a husband and two sons. You don't need to remember the names of the men because—spoiler alert—all three of them die.

Naomi's family found themselves in enemy territory. These were the days of the judges, and political tensions

6. LISTENING

were high. Think of Israel during this period as the wild west. This family had resigned itself to live in self-imposed exile for the rest of their days. After the father died, the sons decided to settle down and marry Moabite women. One wife was named Orpah (not to be confused with Oprah), and the other was named Ruth.

Over the next decade, the two sons also died. Naomi grieved the loss of her husband and children. The three widows were left to fend for themselves. There weren't the same kind of opportunities for women to go out and start a career in the ancient world. A widow had three options: remarry, be taken in, or be poor.

Naomi knew she was past her prime. The famine in Judah ended, so she decided to go back to Judah and perhaps live off the mercy of a relative. Ruth and Orpah still had a shot at remarrying. To spare them the hardship of trying to start over in a foreign land, Naomi begged her two daughters-in-law to stay in Moab. Orpah understood Naomi's logic and went her own way. Ruth, on the other hand, displayed fierce loyalty with her response.

> "For where you go I will go, and where you lodge I will lodge. Your people shall be my people, and your God my God. Where you die I will die, and there will I be buried. May the LORD do so to me and

more also if anything but death parts me from you." (Ruth 1:16-17)

There's no arguing with a speech like that. Ruth would rather take her chances as a widow with Naomi than face life without her. Together they journeyed back to Bethlehem just in time for the barley harvest. Fortunately, God built provision for the poor into the law by requiring Jews to leave the edges of the field untouched for the poor or the foreigner (Leviticus 19:9-10). Ruth was both. Ruth spent all day out in the hot sun gathering as many ears of grain as she could hold. She hardly took a break all day. The owner of the field was a man named Boaz. Something about Ruth caught his eye. When he found out that she left her home in Moab to seal her fate with Naomi, he was doubly impressed.

Boaz approached Ruth and told her not to glean grain from anyone else's field. She could work right alongside his servants. His men would protect her, and she had full access to their water if she got thirsty. Boaz shared his bread and wine at dinner time and even sent her home with some roasted grain. You might not pick up on it, but Boaz is totally flirting. Can you feel the sparks flying?

When Ruth came home later that night, Naomi wanted to know everything. *Who's the lucky guy?* When

6. LISTENING

Naomi found out Ruth hit it off with Boaz, she was ecstatic! Boaz was a close relative of Elimelech (Naomi's late husband). If anyone redeemed their family line, it would be him.

Ruth took Boaz up on his invitation to glean in his field throughout the whole harvest season. Just as the harvest was coming to a close, Naomi hatched a plan. She told Ruth to shoot her shot. Naomi instructed Ruth to bathe and wear perfume and her cloak instead of her work clothes to the threshing floor. The next step was to find where Boaz was sleeping and lie down at his feet. Boaz would take it from there. Bold move.

Ruth replied, "All that you say I will do" (Ruth 3:5). That night, Ruth followed Naomi's directions exactly. Boaz was startled awake to find a young woman curled up around his feet. This experience was equal parts pleasant and unsettling for him. As if it wasn't clear what Ruth's intentions were, she was leaving no room for doubt. She told him, "I am Ruth, your servant. Spread your wings over your servant, for you are a redeemer" (Ruth 3:9). Boaz was flattered by Ruth's proposition. He would love to marry Ruth, but there was one hang-up. He knew of another man who was a closer relative of Elimelech than himself. This guy had first rights to the family land and the responsibility to take care of any remaining family members. Boaz agreed to redeem her so long as he could convince this guy to give up his right.

The next day, Boaz took care of business. He sat at the city gates, watching and waiting until the next of kin showed up. After a short meeting, Boaz was able to maneuver himself as the redeemer. They swapped a sandal and sealed the deal. Boaz bought the land and married Ruth. Before too long, Ruth gave birth to a son named Obed. "He was the father of Jesse, the father of David" (Ruth 4:17). Ruth went from a widow in a foreign land to the great-grandmother of King David. As if that isn't impressive enough, she is one of the few women listed in the genealogy of Jesus Christ (Matthew 1:5). What's also remarkable about Ruth is that there wasn't anything remarkable about her. She was loyal, and she listened. Yet these characteristics contain the hidden potential for God to do incredible things.

LEARNING TO LISTEN

Find wise people. Listening is helpful only if you are listening to the right people. Especially when you are young, you need mentors and coaches who can point you in the right direction. Some voices are better than others. Ruth was fortunate to have a trustworthy source in Naomi.

6. LISTENING

I was nineteen years old when I asked Mr. Cornett to mentor me. He was my Greek professor and a brilliant scholar. He would teach Bible classes by reading straight from the Greek New Testament instead of an English translation. What stuck out to me was how humble he was.

So, during my sophomore year of college, I asked if he would meet with me once a week. In our first meeting in his office, he asked what I hoped to get out of our time together. I had no idea. I just knew having a mentor was a good thing to do. It turned out that having a mentor was more complicated than I thought.

Mr. Cornett suggested I write out a list of life questions for him. Each week we would discuss one question. We covered dating, marriage, parenting, ministry, finances, discouragement, prayer, doubts, and many more. Sophomore year was my crash course in mentorship, and I couldn't have asked for a better guide.

The best way to determine whether someone is wise or not is to look at their fruit. I'm not talking about apples and bananas. I'm talking about looking at a person's life and discerning if you want to become like them. Do they have healthy relationships? Are they someone with proven character? How happy are they?

The world tends to measure external metrics of success: money, beauty, popularity, status, etc. Don't

WHAT ARE YOU WAITING FOR?

be deceived. Not that these measurements disqualify someone from being a role model. These just aren't as important as the internal qualities.

A tried-and-true list of desirable characteristics is the fruit of the Spirit from Galatians 5:22-23. Use this checklist to look for a mentor:

Love. *Do they give without expecting to be repaid?*
Joy. *Do other people smile when around them?*
Peace. *Do they create harmony in relationships?*
Patience. *How long does it take before they get angry?*
Kindness. *Do they treat people (even strangers) well?*
Goodness. *Are they adding good to the world?*
Faithfulness. *Can you trust them?*
Gentleness. *Are they easy to be around?*
Self-control. *How disciplined are they?*

You won't meet anyone (except Jesus) who exemplifies all these perfectly. But if you find someone who scores well on this list, get to know them better. They are someone you should spend more time around. Buy them coffee and ask them good questions. Some of these relationships will remain casual and occasional, while others become more structured and official.

Follow through with action. Good advice won't do you any good if you ignore it. You have to follow

6. LISTENING

through. Remember Ruth's response to Naomi, "All that you say I will do."

She didn't say, "I'll think about it" or, "That's an interesting perspective."

> **GOOD ADVICE WON'T DO YOU ANY GOOD IF YOU IGNORE IT.**

She said, "I'll do it."

Wise counsel is a gift. Hearing it and doing nothing is like getting a Christmas present and never taking it out of the box. Listeners must be open enough to hear and humble enough to obey.

In my junior year of college, I met weekly with Dr. Whittaker. My friendship with Dr. Whittaker spanned beyond college, so now I call him by his first name, John. Often, John would give me not only advice, but challenges. Our meetings came with homework. On one occasion, we talked about the relationship between self-control and fasting. The next thing I knew, I was fasting once a week.

Another meeting sticks out in my mind. I was talking to John about a girl I was interested in (it was Shaina). Except I wasn't sure how much I liked her at that point. We hadn't had the "define the relationship" talk yet. I kept going back and forth about the pros and cons of talking to Shaina about my feelings.

WHAT ARE YOU WAITING FOR?

Finally, John said, "Josh, you are being way too logical about all this. You either like her or you don't. You're not Spock from Star Trek. Just talk to her."

I knew John was right, but I didn't realize it until he said it. Mentors can help you process what is going on inside of you. They offer a much-needed outside perspective on your life. By the end of the week, Shaina and I had our first talk about our relationship.

If you feel that someone is giving you good advice, you should listen to it even if it isn't always what you want to hear. A good mentor may confront you about sin and challenge you to grow. Don't get defensive. Just listen. You might not like it at the moment, but looking back later, you will be glad for the rebuke. Proverbs 27:6 says it well, "Faithful are the wounds of a friend; profuse are the kisses of an enemy."

Hold plans loosely. One of the most significant reasons we don't listen to other people is that we hold onto our plans too tightly. We have our destination in mind, and we are sticking to it. We will be more open to listening when we hold our plans loosely.

Contrary to what many think, most people don't know exactly where they are going. We set goals and do our best to stick to the plan, but inevitably things change. One of my favorite examples of going with the flow is singer-songwriter Jack Johnson.

6. LISTENING

Johnson grew up in Hawaii, where he developed a deep love for surfing. By his teens, he was competing professionally in surfing competitions. He had a promising future riding waves until a severe surfing accident changed the course of his life. During his recovery, he turned to music as a way to pass the time, practicing guitar and writing songs.

Initially, Johnson's music was a hobby, but his passion for it grew steadily. He started recording his music, and by the late 90s, his mellow acoustic sound soon caught the attention of others. He released his breakthrough album, *Brushfire Fairytales,* in 2001, and his career in music only built momentum from there (12 million monthly Spotify listeners isn't too bad).

I listened to Jack Johnson's melodies countless times in high school. His songs are the essence of chill vibes. We probably would have never heard songs like "Better Together" or "Banana Pancakes" if Johnson held his plans too tightly. Instead of letting his accident keep him down for good, Johnson traded his surfboard for a guitar. It turns out that navigating life's unexpected twists and turns can be a lot like riding a wave.

Ruth probably didn't expect to marry into a family where her husband, brother-in-law, and father-in-law all died within ten years. She never thought she would move across the Jordan River to the small Judean town of Bethlehem. None of this was part of her plan. In hindsight, she could tell it was God's plan.

AVERAGE LISTENING

Always be ready to pivot. *Pivot* was a buzzword in 2020. When the COVID-19 pandemic hit, everyone was talking about pivoting. Overnight, restaurants had to figure out online ordering and delivery. Churches streamed their services on social media. Teachers taught students on Zoom.

In sports like basketball, a pivot is where a player changes directions while keeping one foot planted on the ground. It opens up more opportunities to pass or score without moving to a different place on the court.

I'm only 5'6", so I didn't play much basketball growing up. Instead, I played soccer. I can tell you that one of the best skills on the field is communication. The best team players are always listening to where their teammates are. They hear warnings that a defender is coming up behind them. When things go south, listening will allow you to change directions.

The summer after my junior year in college, I was all set to do an internship at a church in the rural town of Kuna, Idaho. I had served at the same church in Boise for three years and was looking for exposure to other

6. LISTENING

ministry contexts. I got along well with the pastor at this other church, and it seemed like a good fit to me. Danny didn't see it that way.

Even though I wasn't meeting with Danny as an "official" mentor yet, I still valued his gems of good advice. In a passing conversation in the hallway, he asked about my summer plans. I told him about Kuna.

Instead of being excited for me, Danny said, "Seems like you've got a good thing going at the church you are currently at. It'd be a shame to lose out on everything you've built up there just because you want to go somewhere new."

After that mic drop, Danny walked off. I was left standing there puzzled. Everyone else I talked to about the internship seemed thrilled. What did Danny know, anyway?

That same afternoon Marcus called. He was the pastor I would be interning under. He explained that it didn't seem like the internship was going to work out. The church didn't have any money in the budget to pay me. Kuna was a half-hour drive away, and I didn't have a car. The deal-breaker was that Marcus himself would be away on a mission trip for several weeks over the summer.

WHAT ARE YOU WAITING FOR?

"I'm sorry this is falling through last minute," Marcus apologized. "I hope you can find another place to intern this summer."

I was shocked, but thanks to Danny I wasn't surprised. I phoned up the youth pastor at the church I was currently serving. I asked if the church could offer me an official summer internship that I needed for school. He was excited about the idea.

After talking with the leadership team, the church offered me a part-time job. I continued to pour into the students I had been with for the last three years. The job turned into a full-time ministry position the week after I graduated college. Maybe Danny knew what he was talking about after all.

You might be a quarter-turn away from your best decision ever. In sports, you don't pivot once in a season, but dozens of times every game. Keep your ears sharp. Don't waste your time trying to force open a door that God has closed. If you do, you'll miss out on the open door just down the hallway.

Know when not to listen. Good listening doesn't mean you say "yes" every time. People-pleasers do whatever others say because they don't want to let anyone down. As a result, they let everyone down. They are like a piece of driftwood, tossed to and fro by every

6. LISTENING

opinion that comes their way. That kind of life is a recipe for disaster.

Wisdom knows when to listen and when not to. We should ignore the advice of foolish or wicked people. (Don't do drugs, kids.) Beyond the obvious stuff, we must also discern times to graciously set aside guidance from those closest to us.

Ruth disregarded Naomi's plea to leave her. Naomi's argument was logical. Ruth was still young, and she'd have a much better chance of remarrying in her home country. Mother-in-law knows best, right?

At that moment, Ruth displayed not only fierce loyalty but also disobedience. She knew that Naomi needed her help, whether she would admit it or not. She knew Naomi was speaking from a place of deep pain. Her plan to go back to Judea alone has the same tone as someone who says, "Just leave me to die!" Ruth called Naomi's bluff and recognized that this was a rare occasion where it was best not to listen.

No one person is infallible. Even our greatest heroes are wrong from time to time. Danny shows up in so many of my examples because I truly value his opinion so highly. But I haven't always followed his advice blindly. One moment in particular comes to mind.

I was in the first mile of a run when I bumped into Danny out on the trail. We both exercise frequently and live in the same part of town, so this happens from time to time. I stopped for a moment to chat with him. I was right in the thick of praying and processing about the merger between Hill City Church and Capitol City Christian Church.

I asked Danny what he thought about the merger. He wasn't so sure about it. He brought up some good points to consider. A merger would change our church culture. It could be challenging to integrate two completely different groups of people. An older, established congregation might say they want the fresh energy of our young church now, but later not fully accept the change we would bring. Then there was the building. It needed a ton of work and would be exhausting to renovate.

"I'll pray that you make the right decision," Danny said as we parted ways.

I had lots to think about for the rest of my run. Ultimately, Danny was right about many of his hesitations with the merger. In many ways, it was more difficult than I had ever realized it would be. However, Danny wasn't part of the meetings I was having with the Capitol City elders. They were 100% on board. The whole process felt like we were in a boat rowing the same direction.

6. LISTENING

I didn't ignore Danny's advice. I listened and learned from his perspective, but I wasn't persuaded by that conversation either. You are going to encounter situations like this one. Even when you think a mentor might be wrong, they will help you clarify the best decision. It forces you to solidify the "why" behind what you are doing. In these moments, respectfully disagree with the person you respect.

Arrive at unexpected destinations. My life today looks drastically different than the life I had planned for myself. That's the beautiful thing about listening to the leading of the Spirit and the wisdom of great people; you never know where you will end up .

I never thought I would settle down in Boise.

From the moment I moved to Idaho, I didn't see what the fuss was all about. For a place called "the city of trees," I was shocked by how few trees there were. Don't get me wrong—there are plenty of trees in the actual city. But the foothills surrounding Boise are dry as a bone.

YOU NEVER KNOW WHERE YOU WILL END UP.

Keep in mind I'm from Alaska. Around half the state (10.9 million acres) is forest land. When I moved to Boise, I felt like Bilbo Baggins in *The Fellowship of the Ring* saying, "I want to see mountains again, Gandalf. Mountains!"

WHAT ARE YOU WAITING FOR?

I always pictured myself moving to some hip metropolitan city like Portland or Seattle to plant a church. I even tried moving once or twice. Each time, something (or someone) kept me in Boise.

I never thought I would be a campus pastor at an established church. You've probably heard stories of churches starting in living rooms and growing from there. A couple reasons for this are that the leader can experiment and has complete influence over the direction. Starting from scratch is what I thought I wanted. I certainly didn't aspire to take a leadership position at an established church.

In 2017, I felt like God called me to move into a campus pastor role at the church that I had been at for eight years. The Holy Spirit made this transition clear to both Shaina and me. We listened even though we didn't understand it at the time. A year and a half later, things finally made sense when we had the opportunity to plant Hill City Church.

I never thought I would participate in a church merger. In a church planting class at Bible college, I met a guy named Bob. The professor brought him in to share his experience in the church planting world. He wasn't like the other church planters. His sending organization had assigned him to a dying congregation. He was working to bring the church back from the brink

6. LISTENING

of closing. I went out to lunch with him and decided that church revitalization was far too much work.

Never say never. Staying in Boise, relaunching Hill City Church, and merging with Capitol City were never part of my plan. Looking back, I'm so glad I didn't get what I thought I wanted. God's plan is always better. Nowadays, I get to work at a thriving church in downtown Boise. I pinch myself from time to time to make sure that I'm not dreaming.

You may not always see where the road ends up. That's okay; God does. His ways are higher than our ways. Keep listening to him. Listen to the wise people he puts in your path. Eventually, you'll end up at the exact place you never knew you wanted to be.

THINK ABOUT IT

Growth takes time. Before you move on, slow down long enough to reflect, journal, or discuss these questions:

1. What do you need advice about in your life right now? Where do you usually turn for answers (internet, friends, parents, yourself)?
2. How good are you at discerning good advice from bad? What would help you get better?

WHAT ARE YOU WAITING FOR?

3. Who is a wise person that you would like to learn from? What about their life do you want to replicate? What would it look like to spend more time listening to that person?
4. How do you usually respond when someone gives you feedback that you didn't want to hear? What would help you receive criticism better?
5. Is there any advice that you have received but feel like you shouldn't listen to? Why not? How can you cross-check your gut to make sure you are on the right track?
6. How adaptable are you when plans change? Are there any directions in which you need to pivot your plans for the future?

7
INNOVATION

"The chief enemy of creativity is good sense."
—*Pablo Picasso*

I'm a true child of the '90s. I grew up on a steady diet of Cap'n Crunch, Saturday morning cartoons, and Super Nintendo. The Scholastic Bookfair was the highlight of the school year. We traded Beanie Babies and Pokémon cards because we were confident they would be worth millions one day (we were wrong).

I'm just old enough to remember a world without WIFI and cell phones. Technology back then seems like dinosaurs compared to today. We didn't have access to game apps, social media, and distractions every second of every day. Entertainment wasn't on-demand. You had

WHAT ARE YOU WAITING FOR?

to wait until after the commercial break to see if Batman would beat the bad guy.

A truly classic experience of the '90s was going to Blockbuster Video. I can still visualize the rows of VHS tapes reminding patrons to "be kind, rewind." My family visited Blockbuster as a weekly ritual. We would return the previously rented videos to avoid the steep late fees. While we were there, we would rent a combination of new releases and classics for the week ahead. If my brother and I were lucky, we'd even get to pick out a snack at the checkout.

Once upon a time, Blockbuster dominated the video rental scene. In its heyday, there were more than 9,000 stores. Today, one lonely Blockbuster video store exists. This outdated relic of the past still stands as a novelty destination in Bend, Oregon.

Blockbuster had thousands of locations, millions of customers, and billions of dollars. On paper, they had every ingredient for success. How did this entertainment giant fall? One word: Netflix.

Netflix started as a mail-delivery DVD service. They offered an alternative to the traditional brick-and-mortar video rental experience. Co-founder Reed Hastings had the idea for the business when Blockbuster slammed him with a $40 late fee.[24] Little did they know they created their own nemesis.

7. INNOVATION

Netflix isn't the only reason why Blockbuster filed for bankruptcy in 2010. Competition is a reality of business. Consumer habits often shift in our ever-changing world. The real reason why Blockbuster died is that it failed to innovate. What got them to the top wasn't going to take them any further. They didn't adapt when they needed to the most.

Netflix, on the other hand, is a shining example of innovation. Innovators find new and better ways to do things. Pastor Craig Groeschel clarifies an important point about innovation: "People with ideas are not innovators. People who follow through with ideas are innovators."[25] It could be a slight tweak to what you are currently doing or a brand-new discovery altogether. Contrary to what you might think, innovation is not an accident that you stumble upon. It is a skill that grows when you use it. We all can find new things that work.

Netflix is my favorite example of innovation because it kept trying new things over time. The following timeline of significant dates comes from "The Story of Netflix" on Netflix.com.[26]

- In 1997, co-founders Reed Hastings and Marc Randolph sent themselves a DVD in the mail. Initially, they thought about VHS (which was still popular at the time), but the slim design of the

WHAT ARE YOU WAITING FOR?

DVD worked better for postage. It worked! After the DVD arrived in one piece, they launched a website, and away they went.

- In 1999, Netflix switched to a subscription-based model. Today you can get a subscription for virtually anything, but in the '90s, this model was a rarity. Netflix also did away with late fees and allowed customers to rent an unlimited number of DVDs. These decisions shook things up significantly for traditional video rental services like Blockbuster.
- In 2007, Netflix introduced a limited selection of TV series and movies directly streamed to customers. Few devices existed at that point that could stream movies to a TV. Technological roadblocks didn't stop Netflix. They saw into the future and created a brand-new way to consume entertainment.
- The new video-streaming company dipped its toes into creating original content in 2012. It started with a stand-up comedy special with comedian Bill Burr. The following year, Netflix was producing original series like *Arrested Development* and *House of Cards* (which won three Emmy awards). A former DVD rental website was now competing with the likes of significant TV broadcasting networks.

7. INNOVATION

These moments represent significant innovation milestones for Netflix. There are also more minor ways that the company is always trying to move things forward. The Marvel/Netflix series "Daredevil" included audio descriptions for the visually impaired. Choice-based episodes allowed viewers to determine the outcome of the story with the click of a button. Even in these small experiments, you can see a culture of innovation alive and well in Netflix today.

Unfortunately, the older we get, the more like Blockbuster we become. We get set in our ways. Maybe you have accomplished some level of success, and you're afraid trying something new will jeopardize everything. We wrongly believe that doing the same thing forever will continue to work. It won't.

WE GET SET IN OUR WAYS.

The real tragedy of Blockbuster is that it used to practice innovation. Their barcode system was state of the art, allowing a store to track up to 10,000 titles. Former CEO David Cook built a $6 million distribution center which allowed the company to outpace any mom-and-pop store in town. Over time, video games and music were added to the inventory to expand the customer base.

WHAT ARE YOU WAITING FOR?

Blockbuster started with innovation—but didn't stick with it. They became comfortable and complacent with their success. It didn't have to end this way. Along the steady decline, there were numerous opportunities that the executives could have taken. They considered buying a cable TV network and opening a theme park. Blockbuster was even working with Enron to develop the first wide-scale, on-demand, video-streaming service.[27] Each time, they chose to maintain the status quo. In 2000, Blockbuster had the opportunity to buy Netflix for $50 million. Netflix is now worth over $230 billion. To rub salt in the wounds, Netflix released an original documentary titled "The Last Blockbuster" in 2020.

All of us have a choice to be like Netflix or Blockbuster. The world is changing all around us. The peer pressure to do what everyone else is doing is intense. We can go with the flow and maintain the status quo. Or we can see things with fresh eyes and challenge the norm.

DANIEL: REBEL CAPTIVE

Daniel grew up in one of the most tumultuous periods in ancient history. The Babylonian empire was on the rise. Judah had forsaken God and his ways for generations. Finally, God's patience wore thin, and wrath was coming.

7. INNOVATION

The prophet Jeremiah delivered a message of impending doom: "This whole land shall become a ruin and a waste, and these nations shall serve the king of Babylon seventy years" (Jeremiah 25:11).

Daniel was a young teenager when King Nebuchadnezzar sent his troops into Jerusalem. Babylon wouldn't lay waste to the Jewish capital for another twenty years, but the journey into captivity had begun. Young Israelite nobles, including Daniel, were taken back to Babylon for assimilation.

Nebuchadnezzar's goal was total cultural indoctrination. He wanted the children of conquered nations to learn the ways of the empire. Babylon would give them the best and the brightest leadership roles. It would be easier to control people when they feel like they have representation in the palace. If displaced Jews ever doubted the goodness of the empire, the king could point to their healthy, educated youths as examples of Babylon's benevolence. Propaganda at its finest.

Babylonian brainwashing included three components.

Step one: Education. Daniel learned the language and literature of Babylon (Daniel 1:4). If you want to understand a culture, listen to the stories they tell. The curriculum in Babylon was highly pagan. High achievers would graduate to become magicians and sorcerers

WHAT ARE YOU WAITING FOR?

(think voodoo, not Harry Potter). The program lasted three years. Any Christian who attends a highly secular college knows how difficult it can be to keep faith in a hostile environment. Still, it is possible. Daniel learned how to listen and answer correctly without believing everything Babylonian instructors told him. He could list the name of every pagan god but still worship Yahweh as the name above every other name.

Step two: Lifestyle. Court officials like Ashpenaz ensured that captive kids learned the Babylonian way of life. Imagine having to learn a radically different culture: new clothes, new entertainment, new food. My family moved to Australia when I was 16 years old. One unexpected aspect of culture shock I experienced was not finding the same foods I was used to at the grocery store. *(What do you mean they don't sell Cap'n Crunch?!)*

For Daniel and his Israelite friends, the Babylonian diet was problematic. They weren't gluten-free or anything like that. The problem was dietary restrictions in the Jewish law. God had commanded his covenant people to adhere to strict food laws (see Leviticus 11 and Deuteronomy 14).

Babylonians, on the other hand, could eat all the bacon and shellfish they wanted. Things got even more complicated when Daniel found out meals would primarily be meat and wine from the king's table. The

7. INNOVATION

king's menu might sound nice, but servants offered the food to pagan idols before consumption. Dodging this dilemma was more difficult than skating through school with passing grades. You can only miss so many meals before you starve.

Step three: Identity. Finally, the Babylonians gave Daniel and his fellow Israelites new names. Nicknames may not seem like a big deal to us. But in the ancient world, your name represented who you were. A name revealed your identity and even pointed to your destiny.

Daniel means, "Elohim is my judge." The name he was given is Belteshazzar, meaning "May Bel protect his life."[28] *Elohim* is a Hebrew name for God, and Bel is a false god. Daniel's Israelite friends, Hananiah, Mishael, and Azariah, were renamed Shadrach, Meshach, and Abednego. Each of their new names also included Babylonian deities. Pastor Rodney Stortz explains the thought process of the king:

> "The Babylonians changed the Hebrew teens' names in an attempt to make them forget the true God and change their worship, but it appears throughout the entire book that Daniel never did forget the name he was given, which honored the true God."[29]

WHAT ARE YOU WAITING FOR?

How did Daniel resist the crushing pressure of Babylon? He had only two options at a glance: disobey the king and probably die, or disobey God (never a good idea). Daniel looked past the obvious and saw a third option. He learned to innovate. What if there was a way to obey God and not die? It was worth a shot.

Daniel's bright idea was to hold an eating contest (not hot dogs). Daniel and his friends would consume nothing but vegetables and water for ten days. The rest of the youths in the palace would eat the king's food. At the end of the challenge, Ashpenaz would measure the two groups against one another. If the Israelites looked just as healthy as the rest of the students, they would be allowed to be vegetarians.

The cost of this kind of challenge was high. If Daniel couldn't bulk up on rice and beans, he was putting himself and his friends in danger. At best, they would suffer disgrace for losing a contest. At worst, they could face death. Even the court official that Daniel bargained with was afraid of decapitation for disobeying Nebuchadnezzar's strict orders. If it weren't for God's favor on Daniel, the contest would have never taken place.

Ten days passed, and it was time for the big weigh-in. Daniel and his friends looked great! They were healthier than the crew that ate red meat and drank

7. INNOVATION

alcohol (surprise, surprise). I guess my mom was right all those times she told me to eat my veggies.

This moment was a turning point in Daniel's life. He refused to compromise his faith, and God blessed him for it. God grew these four friends in wisdom and stature. They graduated at the top of their class, and Nebuchadnezzar favored them above their peers.

> **HE REFUSED TO COMPROMISE HIS FAITH.**

God specially gifted Daniel to interpret visions and dreams. Daniel didn't dabble in the worldly divination of the Babylonians. God had given him spiritual sight. He was able to see what nobody else could. When Nebuchadnezzar had a bad dream, Daniel was the only one in the kingdom who knew what it meant. When Nebuchadnezzar's successor Belshazzar saw writing on the wall, Daniel was the only one who could read it. Using this gift, he rose to one of the most recognized leaders in the empire.

Later in life, Daniel defied an empire once again. He was in his eighties, and the Persians had replaced the Babylonians as the world superpower. King Darius was on the throne, and Daniel was one of his favorite officials. He promoted Daniel to one of the top positions

WHAT ARE YOU WAITING FOR?

in the kingdom. The other officials were jealous and hatched a plot to remove Daniel from the equation.

They knew Daniel was fiercely loyal to his God. They drafted a royal decree stating that no one could pray to any god or man other than the king for thirty days. Darius signed the papers effective immediately. If anyone broke the thirty-day mandate, guards would throw him into the lion's den. (Keeping a den of hungry lions as an execution method is a total evil-villain move.)

Daniel faced another dilemma. He had managed to stay faithful to God for decades in exile. He wasn't about to stop worshipping God now. On the flip side—lions. Instead of panicking or caving, he kept courage and prayed despite the danger. It didn't take long for his enemies to catch him in the act. They swiftly arrested Daniel and threw him to the wild beasts. The tragic loss of his favorite advisor deeply grieved King Darius. Even though Darius was the king, he couldn't reverse the decree. Rules are rules.

That night Darius didn't eat or sleep. He was sick to his stomach thinking about Daniel's fate. The following day he ran to roll the stone away. He called out to Daniel, hoping for a miracle. To everyone's surprise, Daniel was alive!

God had sent an angel to shut the mouths of the lions. Daniel made it out alive "because he had trusted

7. INNOVATION

in his God" (Daniel 6:23). Prayer is what sent him to the lions, and prayer is what saved him. Daniel always stayed relentlessly faithful to God. When faced with dilemmas, danger, and death, he stayed strong. Every time Daniel was boxed in from the world, he used his spiritual sight to see another way out. You can learn to see the world like Daniel did, too.

LEARNING INNOVATION

Forget (some of) what you know. Something called "the curse of knowledge" is our primary barrier to innovation. Doug Paul explains it like this: "It's like we can't see beyond our suddenly limited vantage point of how to do something quite differently."[30] Sometimes knowledge gets in the way of seeing correctly.

A person who has been doing a task the same way for thirty years typically can't imagine a different way of doing it. On the one hand, familiarity with the job is what makes this person efficient. At the same time, they are almost incapable of learning a new way. Knowledge is both a blessing and a curse.

To use another illustration, imagine giving someone directions from your house to your favorite restaurant. You might list prominent street names, highlight landmarks, or get fancy using words like "east" and

WHAT ARE YOU WAITING FOR?

"west." To your surprise, their eyes glaze over, and they have no idea what you are talking about. How could they be so ignorant?

And perhaps they are ignorant. Your friend hasn't driven that route dozens of times like you have. You may know how to get to the taco truck (or pizza place, or burger joint, etc.) the same way every time. You've probably worn tire tracks into the street. You could drive there in your sleep.

Similarly, we develop neural pathways in our minds that help us spend less thinking power on doing the same things we've done before. Craig Groeschel describes neural pathways as the ruts formed on muddy roads. He references one road sign in Alaska that reads, "Choose your rut carefully. You'll be in it for the next sixty miles."[31] Growing up in Alaska, I can say that this is hardly an exaggeration.

When it comes to innovation, ignorance can be a good thing. When you don't have as many ruts in your mind, you are free to go where you please. It frees a person from the curse of knowledge. Unlike you, your friend might drive an unconventional route to the restaurant. They may take some detours that aren't as efficient. But in the process, they might just find a better or more scenic way.

7. INNOVATION

Young people are inclined to innovate because they don't know everything yet. You don't know what you don't know. Your lack of experience allows you to have an outside perspective on problem solving. You can walk into a situation and intuitively say, "Why don't you try it like this?" Whereas a person who is too close likely can't see it any other way. It's possible that Daniel had no trouble suggesting a vegetarian diet because he was the new kid on the block.

If you have been working in a field for more than a year or two, you'll need to learn to forget some of what you know. Try approaching a problem like it is your first day on the job. Put yourself in the shoes of someone else who has no idea about your industry. Try explaining what you are working on to a toddler. These are all thought experiments that help you see your problem from a different point of view.

When in doubt, you can always get an actual differing viewpoint by inviting input from an outsider. Too many leadership teams ask the experts when they should be asking the rookies. Search out people with little to no experience and do a brainstorming session. It may feel like everyone is throwing spaghetti at the wall. But eventually, one of those noodles is going to stick.

Try crazy things. Experimentation is a necessary part of innovation. You'll never have a breakthrough

WHAT ARE YOU WAITING FOR?

if your ideas stay on paper. Imagine Daniel trying to convince Ashpenaz with a point-by-point PowerPoint presentation. He knew he'd never win an argument with a high-ranking Babylonian official. He's just a kid. So Daniel got creative and suggested an experiment.

Growing up, I always loved the science fair. Dioramas and trifold displays still bring back fond memories. Throughout elementary school, I came up with creative experiments, but the blue ribbon always eluded me. Then in the sixth grade, I finally won first prize. My experiment? Potato chips.

I hypothesized that organic potato chips are just as greasy as Lay's brand. I began my research by comparing the nutrition facts on the back of two bags. Then I selected similar-sized chips and placed them on napkins. After a few days of soaking up oil, the results were in. I mapped out the surface area of grease using a grid pattern. My conclusion—the two kinds of chips are equally greasy!

You have suspicions that will remain a mystery until you try them. Your hypothesis might be wrong. That's okay. It's why they call it an educated *guess*. The Netflix co-founders would've never made it big if their mail-in DVD business idea stayed on the whiteboard. What did they do? They popped a DVD in the mail. If it showed up shattered in pieces, they would have tried

7. INNOVATION

something else. All the experiment cost them was the price of a stamp.

Stop talking and start trying. If you have the thought, "I wonder what would happen if I…" then it's time to experiment. It's not complicated; we learned this stuff in elementary school. Make an educated guess and test it. Don't expect to be correct, and don't assume that if it works once, it will work again. If you commit to the process, your idea will become more refined over time. Eventually, you might even come up with something great.

Innovation, by definition, is something new. Life.Church has a motto, "To reach people no one is reaching, we'll do things no one is doing."[32] If someone were already doing it, you wouldn't need to experiment. You could simply read about it and implement. The reason there are so many copycats in the world is that trying new things feels intimidating. If you want to get the fruit, you'll need to go out on a limb.

Free yourself to fail. The more successful we become, the more we tend to fear failure. When you are inexperienced, you don't have anything to lose. You haven't built an empire that will fall if you fail. In fact, most people expect youngsters to fail. This expectation frees you up to try something new and shake things up.

WHAT ARE YOU WAITING FOR?

Elon Musk once said, "If you're not failing, you're not innovating enough."[33]

Failure doesn't mean you're losing; it means you are one step closer to winning next time. But you have to fail the right way. We fail forward by learning why something didn't work. When you understand why the science experiment blew up in your face, you'll be able to adjust for the next version. Take the pressure off. You don't have to come up with a million-dollar idea the first go around. If the initial prototype doesn't work, move on to version 2.0 (and 3.0 and 4.0, etc.).

One way you can free yourself to fail is to start small. Too many people expect to hit the nail on the head the first time. Once they get an idea in the hopper, they invest way too much into it. They tell everyone how their idea is the next big thing. They post it all over social media. They recruit every friend and spend every penny. When these ideas fail, they fail big.

If you start small, you can fail small. Try testing out your idea without spending any money. Then when it goes sideways, you can still buy lunch. Instead of telling the world, talk to a few trusted friends. That way, you'll be less likely to let pride push you to hold on to something that's not working. Sometimes things that look great on a whiteboard don't translate well to the real world.

7. INNOVATION

Unfortunately, many innovative leaders lose their creative spark over time. They lose their scrappy attitude from the early years and retreat inside the box. Instead of looking to the future, they become hyper-concerned about maintaining the present. Ironically, the leaders who become too focused on keeping the success they've built often end up plateauing.

It doesn't have to be this way. You can keep trying new things until your dying breath. Daniel did it. He didn't challenge the status quo only as a teenager. He kept going against the grain well into his 80s! The secret is never to get too attached to what success you have. If you want to win, you'll need to keep playing risks when it matters most. Innovation is not something you do once and then never do again. Keep at it, and it will serve you throughout your life.

LEVERAGING INNOVATION

Embrace constraints. Most people see insufficiency as an impossible brick wall. They believe the lie that we can't because we don't have…fill in the blank. As we saw in chapter 3, constraints force us to get creative. Perpetual innovators can welcome limits with open arms.

Craig Groeschel believes this. He says, "Having more isn't always better—it can slow things down,

WHAT ARE YOU WAITING FOR?

make us lazy, or allow us to buy solutions instead of creating them. Limitations are the breeding grounds for innovation."[34]

Instead of asking, "What could we do if we had x, y, z?" start asking, "What can we do with what we have now?"

This question reminds me of cooking in my house growing up. My parents couldn't always afford to stock our pantry with groceries. There were times when money was so tight that my mom would visit the local food bank. She would bring home an eclectic cornucopia of canned food.

Yet my mom always had a great attitude. She would try new recipes and make substitutions if we didn't have the exact right ingredients. "Tonight we're getting creative!" she would say. To be honest, not every dinner was a home run. But we survived and made it through those difficult years.

Even if you find yourself in a land of plenty, you can still embrace constraints. Simply impose limits on yourself. How could you get more done while working fewer hours? How would you double your impact as an organization without adding more staff? How could you make more profit without increasing your budget? These ways of thinking will allow you to get creative even if you don't have to by necessity.

7. INNOVATION

Change the game. What got you where you are likely won't get you where you want to go next. The world around us is constantly changing. Imagine that you sit down to play checkers. A moment later, you look up to see that your opponent has switched the pieces to chess. Just as you are mentally preparing for the different rules of the game, your friend hands you a ping pong paddle. This is our world.

Have you noticed that people who spend their energy trying to stay current are perpetually exhausted? The thing about currents is that they are constantly shifting. What is in one day will be out the next. Instead of going with the flow, you can choose to forge a better path. It is said that the best way to predict the future is to create it.

Innovation allows you to flip the script on your friend and change the game. *You* can be the person who reinvents the rules. Years ago, when I was a youth pastor, we did this all the time. We were always trying to find new ways to help students follow Jesus.

> **OUR YOUTH GROUP WAS A PETRI DISH FOR FRESH IDEAS.**

Our youth group was a petri dish for fresh ideas. Some things worked, and other things didn't. As I look back, there are three game-changing shifts that we made.

WHAT ARE YOU WAITING FOR?

Shift #1: Combining junior high and high school students. We used to run a junior high school program on Wednesdays and high school on Thursdays. At that time, we had two separate staff leaders for each. Then one day, the junior high youth guy got fired. All of a sudden, we had to figure out what to do really quickly. For a time, we tried to continue to run things "business as usual." We became more efficient and taught the same lesson on both nights.

Over time, we realized that we were essentially running the same youth program two nights in a row. That's when we began brainstorming about combining age groups. You would not believe the pushback we got from parents and students (especially the older ones).

Still, we thought we were onto something. We moved forward with a 6th-12th grade youth program. Everyone would be together for hangout, worship, and teaching. Then grades would split up into small groups. There were some bugs to work out, but eventually, we found a new rhythm.

A couple of years after this change, we had more than tripled in size. The high school students who grew up in the ministry started serving in the younger age groups. They knew how impactful it was to have older role models in the church. Instead of disregarding the

7. INNOVATION

young kids, they looked forward to having a positive influence. It changed the game.

Shift #2: Serving at summer camp. Our youth ministry ran four camps per year. All of them used to be essentially the same. We played fantastic games, ran powerful worship experiences, and preached the gospel. One day our strategy shifted when two staff members came back from a youth leader conference.

At a breakout session, they heard from another youth ministry that had canceled youth group. Yes, you read that correctly. This innovative youth ministry realized that they told students all about Jesus but never allowed them to follow Jesus.

So they canceled their big midweek production and did service projects three weeks out of the month. Then the fourth week, they would come together for a worship gathering where they celebrated everything God had done the rest of the month. Surprisingly, they grew in number instead of shrinking. It turns out that young people want to change the world. Who knew?

Although I wasn't present at this conference, the leaders shared an illustration that heavily influenced our youth ministry. Imagine a baseball camp. The coaches sit the students down and give them books to read about baseball. They get a professional baseball player to come and give an inspiring speech about baseball. They even have the kids sing "Take Me Out to the Ball Game." At the end of the camp, they send the kids home—without ever having played baseball. Do you see the problem?

We took this idea and implemented a different kind of summer camp. Instead of renting an expensive venue, students brought sleeping pads and slept on the church building floor for a week. Instead of planning the best activities, we served our city every day. Instead of highly produced sessions, we let students share what God was showing them. We let them play ball for a week. It changed the game.

Shift #3: More Bible study, fewer sermons. Our youth staff went on a day retreat to Twin Falls, Idaho. We were taking time to dream about what it takes to bring youth ministry to the next level. The conversation boiled down to depth in discipleship. We believed that students needed to grow in both their desire and ability to follow Jesus. How could we cultivate depth beyond what we were currently offering in our program?

We landed on a crazy idea. What if we canceled all our youth group sermons for the summer? This method sounded great to me (I was our primary communicator). We would go from worship time straight into small groups. Students would spend extra group time going through an inductive Bible study. We called the series

7. INNOVATION

"Closer." We were banking on James 4:8 being true: "Draw near to God, and he will draw near to you."

I remember the first night of the "Closer" series. I announced that we wouldn't be teaching throughout the summer. As we dismissed to groups, a girl came up to me groaning.

"Why do we have to do this?" she complained.

"Do you like eating out at restaurants?" I questioned.

She hesitantly responded, "Yes…." She had no idea where I was going with this.

"What about a home-cooked meal? Have you ever made one of those?" I continued.

"Yes!" she said.

"Which one do you think is better? The best restaurant you've ever been to or the best home-cooked meal?" I asked.

"Obviously, you can't beat a home-cooked meal," she said. She was starting to get the idea.

"That's right," I concluded. "When you come to church and hear a sermon, it is like going out to a restaurant. Someone else has done all the preparation for you. All you have to do is show up and eat. What we are trying to do this summer is teach you how to feed yourself. We don't want to raise up spiritual consumers; we want to send students out ready to change the world for Jesus."

WHAT ARE YOU WAITING FOR?

"Okay," she skipped away happily.

Each of these three innovations may not sound crazy now, but they changed the game at the time. Although I've been out of youth ministry for years, each of these decisions continues to influence the youth group I used to lead. I was a teenager or in my early twenties for each of these shifts. It won't be easy, but you can change the game, too.

We experienced pushback at the time when we implemented each one. Expect resistance. Remember why you are changing the game. It's not change for the sake of change. It's about change so that you can accomplish your goal more effectively. Identify your desired outcome, and find a better way to get there.

THINK ABOUT IT

Growth takes time. Before you move on, slow down long enough to reflect, journal, or discuss these questions:

1. When it comes to trying new things, are you more like Netflix or Blockbuster? What usually prevents you from experimentation?
2. Do you have any hypotheses or hunches about a better way to do things? What is a step you could take to test your theory?

7. INNOVATION

3. How do you respond to failure? What could you do to free yourself up to fail more?
4. What line of work would you want to revolutionize? What are the problems you can see that currently exist in that industry?
5. What limitations do you face in making progress on your ambitions? For each limit, come up with a creative solution around it.
6. What ideas do you have that would change the game completely? Dream about what the future could look like if your ideas worked.

WHAT ARE YOU WAITING FOR?

CONCLUSION
WHAT ARE YOU WAITING FOR?

The urban artwork scene is strong in Boise. It's one of my favorite things about living here. There is an area downtown called "Freak Alley" where the murals and graffiti are constantly changing.

It's common practice for Boise businesses to paint the side of their buildings to get their message across. One gym has a painting of a muscular man flexing, saying "I love you" to his bicep. Boise CrossFit has printed, "IF NOT TODAY, WHEN?" in massive letters to motivate people to work out. (Imagine driving past that sign while eating a donut.)

That line, "If not today, when?" is really what this book is all about. God has great plans for you today. You don't have to wait to change the world. I hope that you've had people in your life tell you how much they believe in you. If you haven't, let me say it, "I believe in you!" I can be your hype man.

While motivation is important, it's not enough on its own. The statistics show that 80% of people give up on their New Year's resolutions by mid-February.[35] Ambitions without a plan create a recipe for disappointment. Here at the end of this book, I want to give you some final advice for making the most of your life.

BITE-SIZED GOALS

Let's say you have clarity on your life's calling. Hypothetically, let's say you want to go to the moon. That's amazing. But you're not going to the moon tomorrow. So, what happens in between that moon-shot goal and today? Bite-sized goals.

The path to your greatest ambitions is paved with stepping-stone goals that take you in the right direction. Tomorrow you won't get on board a rocket ship, but you can watch a documentary on space travel. You can research astronaut training programs. You could email a real-life astronaut and ask questions about how to get into the space business.

CONCLUSION

I had no idea how to write a book. It was raining for a week on my vacation in Australia, and I was stuck inside. So, I started writing. That was seven years ago. As I sit on my couch writing this conclusion, I can't recall the countless number of bite-sized goals along the way. Here are a few:

I created a reading list of like-minded material and read those books. I watched a video writing class from Malcolm Gladwell. I listened to an audio course by Michael Hyatt on getting published. I created a book proposal, outlined each chapter, and wrote the book. I emailed dozens of high-profile leaders and authors to see if anyone would help promote the book. The list goes on and on.

The point is, every single one of those goals became an item on my checklist. I didn't sit down and write this book in one sitting. It has been years in the making. Most of the significant undertakings we do in life are not instant. They take time and intentionality.

> EVERY SINGLE ONE OF THOSE GOALS BECAME AN ITEM ON MY CHECKLIST.

Something you can do today is sit down and write out ten bite-sized goals that will take you toward your dream. As you check those things off, don't be afraid to add more to the list. If you do this, you'll be well on your way.

GET SPECIFIC

One of the problems with most of our plans is that they aren't specific enough. We say things like, "I want to exercise more" or "I should eat healthier." Those goals are so generic that we are setting ourselves up for failure. Instead, answer these three questions when you plan your goals.

First, what exactly do I want to accomplish? Instead of "exercise more," try "I want to run for thirty minutes three times this week." This kind of goal includes the type of exercise (running), duration (thirty minutes), and deadline (this week). Unless a goal is measurable, you have no way of knowing if you've succeeded or not.

Don't plan on eating *healthier*. Pick which foods you want to eat less of and limit your intake. Decide what foods you want more of in your diet and make a grocery list. Don't just plan on reading the Bible *more*. Pick which book of the Bible and how many chapters you are going to read. The more specific you can be with your "what," the better.

Second, when do I plan on doing it? Important things go in your calendar. If something isn't important

CONCLUSION

enough to get written down, it probably won't get done promptly. Go ahead and block off a time to chip away at your goals.

If you have spiritual goals like growing in your faith, you should schedule a time to read the Bible, pray, and go to church. I wrote more than 90% of this book after 8:00 p.m. Why? It's after my kids go to bed. If I hadn't scheduled it ahead of time, it would never have happened.

Third, where will I be? One step further in setting yourself up for success is to visualize where you will be when you work on your goal. Humans exist in time and space. That means you will be working on your goal at a certain time in a certain place. When you decide ahead of time, it is one less thing to worry about. (I almost always wrote this book on my living room couch.)

When I'm training for a running race, I follow a training plan. It helps to pick which trail or track I'm running at before I leave my house. One day I went to the high school track where I usually run. It was jam-packed with marching band practice. So I drove to another track on the recommendation of a friend. That one was locked. Finally, I went to a third track that I had never been to before. It turns out that the track was actually across the street from the high school where I started. I probably spent an hour figuring out my "where" before I even started on my "what"!

What, when, and where. Remember these three words. If you put your bite-sized goals through the filter of these three questions, you can create a successful plan.

TELL SOMEONE

Accountability is a powerful motivator. Simply knowing that someone else will ask you if you followed through will help you put in the effort. Athletes who post their workouts to an app like Strava are more likely to stay consistent. Why? They know other people will notice.

We implemented game-changing practice in our small group. When we share prayer requests each week, we also share one action step. Our action step can be anything that Jesus is calling us to. It might be from Sunday's sermon, our own devotional time, our small group discussion, or somewhere else. The following week, we share new action steps and follow up on the ones from last time. People rarely fail to follow through on their action step for two weeks straight.

Telling one or two trusted friends will be better accountability than posting your goals on social media. You want to share with people that will check up on

CONCLUSION

you. These are going to be your best cheerleaders when you make progress. They will also be the people who will gently spur you on to get going when you start slacking.

Initially, I didn't tell anyone that I was writing a book. My wife and two dogs were my only witnesses. Guess what? Progress was slow, like painfully slow. When I started getting serious about this book, I told a few more friends. As I wrap up writing, I still haven't posted about it on social media or anything. But these close friends have helped me stay consistent. You need people like this, too.

DO IT ANYWAY

It doesn't take long for resistance to sink in. When you feel like skipping a day, do it anyway. Some days are going to take more willpower than others. If you do miss a day, pick up where you left off tomorrow. Don't try and make up for the lost time. Some progress is better than no progress.

Consistency is more important than intensity. It is better to pray for five minutes every day than for half an hour once a week. Maybe you planned on running three miles but only have time for two. Run two. Keep at it. What takes a ton of willpower now will be a habit in no time.

WHAT ARE YOU WAITING FOR?

Our dreams are like a long journey. You get there one step at a time. It may feel like you are a million miles from where you want to be. I promise that you can make a difference

> CONSISTENCY IS MORE IMPORTANT THAN INTENSITY.

along the way. So, lace up your shoes and walk out the door. Soon you'll look back and see how far you've come. Not every day will be easy, but there will be encouraging moments of realization that will give you the fuel you need to keep going.

10,000 PEOPLE

I sat in the dressing room praying. I had never been in a "dressing room" before. The butterflies were buzzing around my stomach. Usually, I don't feel nervous before preaching, but this time was different. This time I would be preaching to 10,000 people.

I was 28 years old. Somehow, I was asked to be the keynote speaker for a major evangelistic festival in the Treasure Valley. In years past, event organizers booked bands like NEEDTOBREATHE and speakers like Nick Vujicic. This year the budget needed to get cut down substantially. Guess which line item they slashed? (Someone in a meeting said, "I know a young preacher we could get for free!") I was way out of my league.

CONCLUSION

I was honored to get the invitation to share the gospel at an event like this. There is nothing I love more than telling people that Jesus loves them and watching the Holy Spirit bring people into the kingdom of heaven. I love preaching the gospel and calling people to respond in faith.

To be honest, I don't remember too much about the time I was on stage. I spoke for the twenty minutes they allotted me, and then I prayed. It wasn't a life-changing experience for me, but I hope God used it to change someone's life that warm summer night.

This experience is the epitome of how I've tried to spend my youth. I unashamedly walked through any doors that God opened. There were always naysayers and excuses why I needed to wait until I was older. I'm glad I didn't. God grew me through every failure along the way.

I'm not promising that you will be rich and famous if you start leading now. Being rich and famous isn't the point of life anyway. I'm telling you that you can impact the world. If you can make a difference today, why wouldn't you? God created you for such a time as this. Don't waste a moment.

The path ahead will be more challenging than you think. People will tell you that you are too inexperienced, too weak, too young, blah, blah, blah. Who cares? David was too small. Mary was a virgin. Gideon was the weakest

WHAT ARE YOU WAITING FOR?

in his family. Esther was a Jewish girl in a Persian world. Samuel wasn't ordained yet. Ruth was a foreigner and a widow. Daniel was an exile. God has always used young men and women to change the world. He can use you too. What are you waiting for?

NOTES

[1] Kara Powell, Jake Mulder, and Brad Griffin, *Growing Young: Six Essential Strategies to Help Young People Discover and Love Your Church* (Grand Rapids: BakerBooks, 2016), 16.

[2] Craig Groeschel, *Winning the War in Your Mind: Change Your Thinking, Change Your Life* (Grand Rapids: Zondervan, 2021), 20.

[3] Barna Group, "Hopeful Increases: Pastors Are More Optimistic About the Future," *Barna Research,* https://www.barna.com/research/hopeful-increases-pastors/.

[4] Patrick M. Lencioni, *The Ideal Team Player: How to Recognize and Cultivate the Three Essential Virtues: A Leadership Fable* (Hoboken, NJ: Jossey-Bass, 2016), 159.

[5] Jim Collins & Jerry Porras, *Built to Last: Successful Habits of Visionary Companies* (New York: HarperBusiness Essentials, 2002), 91.

[6] Jennifer Davis, "Redefining Work," University of Michigan Alumni Association, https://alumni.umich.edu/michigan-alum/redefining-work/.

[7] Carey Nieuwhof, *Didn't See It Coming: Overcoming the 7 Greatest Challenges That No One Expects and Everyone Experiences* (Colorado Springs: Waterbrook, 2018), 16

[8] Bob Goff, *Dream Big: Know What You Want, Why You Want It, and What You're Going to Do About It* (Nashville: Nelson Books, 2020), 31.

[9] Mark Batterson, *The Circle Maker: Praying Circles Around Your Biggest Dreams and Greatest Fears* (Grand Rapids: Zondervan, 2016), 15.

[10] Bob Iger, "The Importance of Risk-Taking," *Master Class,* https://www.masterclass.com/classes/bob-iger-teaches-business-strategy-and-leadership/chapters/the-importance-of-risk-taking#.

[11] "Charity: Water," https://www.charitywater.org.

[12] Carey Nieuwhof, *Didn't See It Coming,* 74.

[13] Richard Koch, quoted in Andy Stanley, *Next Generation Leader: Five Essentials for Those Who Will Shape the Future* (Sisters, OR: Multnomah Publishers, 2003), 34.

[14] John M. Grohol, "Why Are We Scared of Public Speaking?" *Psychology Today,* November 1, 2017, https://www.psychologytoday.com/us/blog/smashing-

the-brainblocks/201711/why-are-we-scared-of-public-speaking.

[15] Seana Scott, "Esther: Choosing the Right Thing Even When it's the Hard Thing," *Christian Standard,* July 1, 2021, https://christianstandard.com/2021/07/esther-choosing-the-right-thing-even-when-its-the-hard-thing/.

[16] Doug Paul, *Ready or Not: Kingdom Innovation for a Brave New World* (100 Movements Publishing, 2020), 122.

[17] Alex Honnold, "How I Climbed a 3,000-Foot Vertical Cliff—Without Ropes," *TED,* April 2018, https://www.ted.com/talks/alex_honnold_how_i_climbed_a_3_000_foot_vertical_cliff_without_ropes/transcript?language=en.

[18] Liz Wiseman, *Rookie Smarts: Why Learning Beats Knowing in the New Game of Work* (New York: Harper Business, 2014), 18.

[19] John Mark Comer, *The Ruthless Elimination of Hurry: How to Stay Emotionally Healthy and Spiritually Alive in the Chaos of the Modern World* (Colorado Springs: Waterbrook, 2019), 20.

[20] Alex Honnold, "How I Climbed a 3,000-Foot Vertical Cliff—Without Ropes."

[21] Peter and Geri Scazzero, *Emotionally Healthy Relationships: Discipleship That Deeply Changes Your*

Relationship with Others, Workbook and Streaming Video (Grand Rapids: HarperChristian Resources, 2023), 97.

[22] Andy Stanley, *Enemies of the Heart: Breaking Free from the Four Emotions That Control You* (Nashville: Thomas Nelson, 2010), 8.

[23] World Health Organization, *Coronavirus Disease (COVID-19) Situation Report - 13*, February 2, 2020, https://www.who.int/docs/default-source/coronaviruse/situation-reports/20200202-sitrep-13-ncov-v3.pdf.

[24] "How Blockbuster Went from Dominating the Video Business to Bankruptcy," *Business Insider,* August 12, 2020, https://www.businessinsider.com/the-rise-and-fall-of-blockbuster-video-streaming-2020-1.

[25] Craig Groeschel, "The Four Essentials of Innovation," *Life.Church,* https://www.life.church/leadershippodcast/the-four-essentials-of-innovation/#

[26] "About," *Netflix,* https://about.netflix.com/en.

[27] "How Blockbuster Went from Dominating the Video Business to Bankruptcy."

[28] Rodney Stortz, *Daniel: The Triumph of God's Kingdom,* Preaching the Word Commentary (Wheaton: Crossway, 2004), 18.

[29] Rodney Stortz, *Daniel: The Triumph of God's Kingdom,* 18.

[30] Doug Paul, *Ready or Not: Kingdom Innovation for a Brave New World,* 52.

NOTES

[31] Craig Groeschel, *Winning the War in Your Mind: Change Your Thinking, Change Your Life,* 87.

[32] Craig Groeschel, "Anything Short of Sin," *Life.Church,* https://www.life.church/media/jesus-and-we/anything-short-of-sin/.

[33] "For Elon Musk, Failure Is Critical to Success." *Evannex,* March 1, 2023. https://evannex.com/blogs/news/for-elon-musk-failure-is-critical-to-success.

[34] Craig Groeschel, "The Four Essentials of Innovation," *Life.Church Leadership Podcast,* https://www.life.church/leadershippodcast/the-four-essentials-of-innovation/.

[35] Ruth Cohen. "How to Keep Your New Year's Resolutions." *Time,* December 29, 2023. https://time.com/6243642/how-to-keep-new-years-resolutions-2/.

WHAT ARE YOU WAITING FOR?

ACKNOWLEDGEMENTS

I am deeply grateful to Daniel McCoy and the entire team at Renew.org for believing in me and taking a chance on an unknown author. Your unwavering positivity and encouragement have been a constant source of motivation throughout this journey.

I am also thankful for Dale Cornett, John Whittaker, Danny Harrod, and the many other mentors who shaped my early years of leadership. You helped me navigate the challenges of adulthood, steering me away from mistakes and offering grace when I messed up along the way. Your guidance has been invaluable.

A special thanks to Chris Burgess, one of the first people to read the initial manuscript. I'll never forget when you told me this book was worth sharing with the world. Your encouragement and insight into the writing process have been a true gift, and your continued support has meant the world to me.

WHAT ARE YOU WAITING FOR?

To every young person who reads this book—thank you. Your curiosity, your hope, and your courage to imagine a better future inspire me more than you know. I hope this story speaks to your heart and reminds you that God made you for a reason.

Finally, I could not have embarked on this journey without the steadfast love and support of my wife, Shaina. You gave me the space to create, held me up when the road was long, and prayed for this book even in its most uncertain moments. Your faith in me kept me going through every doubt and setback. I am beyond grateful that God brought you into my life.

ABOUT THE AUTHOR

Josh Branham is the Lead Pastor of Hill City Church in Boise, Idaho. He studied preaching at Boise Bible College and later earned his Master of Arts in Christian Ministry from Grand Canyon University.

With over a decade of preaching experience, Josh has developed a unique ability to take complex theological ideas and make them relevant, concrete, and engaging for all audiences. He is passionate about empowering the next generation to discover their God-given gifts and use them for the kingdom. He invests in leaders worldwide, regularly speaking at conferences and creating online content to inspire and equip them to follow Jesus with everything.

When he's not working, Josh enjoys training for marathons, exploring new trails, and spending quality time with his wife, Shaina, and their three daughters. To learn more about Josh and his work, visit www.joshuabranham.com.